Stories of
Deliverance

Stories of Deliverance

Real People Telling Real Stories of Divine Healing

George H. Dawe

Foreword by
Elliott F. Baker
Abbotsford, British Columbia

Edited by
Burton K. Janes
Editor, *Beyond Aslan: Essays on C.S. Lewis*

WESTBOW
PRESS®
A DIVISION OF THOMAS NELSON
& ZONDERVAN

Scripture taken from the Holy Bible, NEW INTERNATIONAL VERSION®. Copyright © 1973, 1978, 1984 by Biblica, Inc. All rights reserved worldwide. Used by permission. NEW INTERNATIONAL VERSION® and NIV® are registered trademarks of Biblica, Inc. Use of either trademark for the offering of goods or services requires the prior written consent of Biblica US, Inc.

WestBow Press books may be ordered through booksellers or by contacting:

WestBow Press
A Division of Thomas Nelson & Zondervan
1663 Liberty Drive
Bloomington, IN 47403
www.westbowpress.com
1 (866) 928-1240

Because of the dynamic nature of the Internet, any web addresses or links contained in this book may have changed since publication and may no longer be valid. The views expressed in this work are solely those of the author and do not necessarily reflect the views of the publisher, and the publisher hereby disclaims any responsibility for them.

Any people depicted in stock imagery provided by Thinkstock are models, and such images are being used for illustrative purposes only. Certain stock imagery © Thinkstock.

ISBN: 978-1-5127-0444-0 (sc)
ISBN: 978-1-5127-0445-7 (hc)
ISBN: 978-1-5127-0443-3 (e)

Library of Congress Control Number: 2015911568

Print information available on the last page.

WestBow Press rev. date: 07/30/2015

This book is

affectionately dedicated
to my esteemed high-school teacher,
Ronald Clarke,
in honour of
his efficient teaching during the 1950s,
his God-conscious approach to life,
his interest in my choosing the right career,
and his warm friendship in demonstrating God's love to others.

Table of Contents

Foreword

George H. Dawe is a pastor, scholar, teacher and writer. He is also my long-time personal friend. We were roommates during our early days of theological training, and colleagues during our many years of pastoral ministry.

George is a prolific writer. I had the privilege of watching this gift develop during our Bible college days. His term papers often secured top grades, and whenever he entered a writing contest 'just for the fun of it,' he usually won an award. So, it didn't surprise me when he was listed in *Who's Who Among Students in American Universities & Colleges 1978-79*.

Writing about biblical characters, George has the unique ability of entering the hearts and souls of his subjects, bringing them astonishingly alive. In his first book, *We Knew Him: Personal Encounters with Jesus of Nazareth*, he writes in the first-person narrative. Now, in *Stories of Deliverance*, he gives his characters a voice of their own. One will smile as George attributes to his characters physical actions and expressions that enliven their particular circumstances. Some examples follow.

Concerning the paralytic and the men preparing to lower him down through the roof, George says, "Then, stretching their backs and wiping the sweat from their brows ...."

In the same story, when Jesus declared "Son, your sins are forgiven," the author visualizes the scribes, the teachers of the Law, "sitting there with furrowed brows and glaring eyes, taking it all in."

The two blind men who were delivered are pictured as following Jesus, tapping their canes and shouting.

Regarding the raising of the widow's son of Nain, heartbroken and grief-stricken by the death of her son, George brings us close to her heart as she expresses her innermost feelings about the throng of people who turned out to grieve with her, "Although their hearts were warm, I felt as if I were wrapped in a cold wet cloak."

Although these expressions are not recorded in the biblical account, they are true to life and add a sense of reality to the characters' stories. Displaying the marks of a serious scholar, George enriches his work with meaningful quotations from various writers.

The author takes us back to Jesus and His healing ministry. However, one does not get the impression that His ministry was meant only for His day. On the contrary, He is still alive and administers healing to many who will believe.

I invite you to read *Stories of Deliverance*. You will receive a fresh understanding of Jesus. As healer and deliverer, He can be your source of deliverance.

Elliott F. Baker
Abbotsford, BC

Introduction

Everyone has a story, a dream, an encounter, an experience. Your story is different from mine, but mine is just as real as yours.

We cherish our stories as valuable enough to save and share. In fact, many of them tell of the miraculous. They report events of God's actions, often transcending the normal operation of natural laws.

Christ's miracles are called *wonders*. By their godly character, they arrest attention and create surprise. They are labelled *mighty works*, because they show superhuman power. And, they are known as *signs*, because they point to a divine mission.

Miracles and stories often teach us lessons, some to show us what to avoid and others to show us what to embrace. They give us opportunities to play leading roles in our daily living, even to fantasize about being the hero or the victim.

Healing of any kind is usually the source of a story – and a good story at that; divine healing more so. That is, to be cured by God's miraculous touch is rare in some cultures; but case after case has been documented and told to the glory of God.

As a boy, I experienced many natural healings for my bruised shins, cut fingers and punctured feet, as well as for mumps and measles. Most of my black eyes were my own fault! And, those of my enemies were my fault, as well!

In Jesus' ministry, He healed people with physical, emotional and spiritual needs. He cured lepers, calmed fevers, raised the dead and delivered the demon possessed. And, through the power of the Holy Spirit, His ministry continues today in families, hospitals and church circles.

The accounts I relate in *Stories of Deliverance* are about real characters in real situations. They show how God heals by His touch and His word, restoring from sickness to health and from death to life. But, best of all, they show Jesus as the Great Physician, the only answer to physical, emotional and spiritual dilemmas.

George H. Dawe

1

Deliverance at a Distance

The Nobleman's Son
John 4:46-54

To be delirious is to be beside oneself. It is the state of delirium, a disordered mind with incoherent speech, sometimes developing from malaria.

This was my son's condition before Jesus healed him. It's the first healing recorded in the New Testament. In fact, only John recorded it. Other miracles had happened in Jerusalem (John 2:23; 3:2), but were not recorded.

Jesus performed miracles because the power to heal resided in Him. His miracles confirmed His deity. When the lame stood and walked, it was a testimony to His divinity. When He drove demons from the possessed, they declared Him to be the Son of God.

My son's healing is recorded as Jesus' second miracle. While His first, turning water into wine, was to bring joy into a marriage, my son's was to bring comfort and hope in times of sickness and sorrow. No doubt Jesus used it to maintain hope in the nation of Israel.

John used the word *sign* to explain Jesus' miracles. Leon Morris says it is "a word which points to the fact that there is spiritual truth demonstrated in the miracles. In the literal sense of the word, miracles are '*sign*ificant.'"

John 12:5 shows that Jesus had a *hands-on* ministry to the poor and needy. Rick Renner comments that "Jesus didn't only perform supernatural works; He also used His resources to do good works in the natural realm. Jesus cared for the poor; He helped feed the needy; and He utilized the vast resources of money made available to His ministry to meet the basic needs of human beings."

What was clear to me was that Jesus knew me and understood my weak faith. According to Him, a man's faith must hinge on the word *believe* — not merely to see signs and wonders, but to accept Jesus as God's Son, and to believe His Word, regardless.

Being a nobleman, I was a Jewish royal official. I lived with my family in Capernaum, a busy fishing port on the Sea of Galilee. As the king's attendant, I was trusted to serve Herod Antipas, ruler over Galilee and Peraea.

Cana was an obscure, out-of-the-way place in the hills of Galilee. It was where Jesus turned the water into wine at a wedding. Because of this, many people, including me, believed Jesus to be a miracle worker.

On this occasion, Jesus had returned to Cana for a visit. At that time, my son was very sick with a seriously high fever. So, out of concern for him, I hurried to Cana to ask Jesus to come down to Capernaum and heal my son. After all, I was the boy's father, and he was dying.

I was not surprised at my son's sickness, but I was devastated. I knew that disease has a way of finding all of us. We may climb a high tower to escape a flood, only to be struck by lightning!

What did Jesus want from me? Faith in Him, even though it was my son who needed healing. Leon Morris points out that "All faith, even that which brings people to Christ for imperfect reasons, is precious before

God ...[T]hough he welcomes all who come, it is better to come in simple trust in Christ for what he is than for the wonders he can perform."

By asking Jesus to come to my house, I figured He could heal only in person or on the spot. I did not realize He could heal from a distance. I mean, how could He heal people without being in their presence? Besides, Cana was sixteen miles from Capernaum.

That was the weakness of my faith. Fortunately, my faith was in the right object. Herbert Lockyer points out, "Faith in a wrong object, no matter how strong, never relieves; but faith in a right object, even although weak, will. It is not faith itself that relieves, but the power of the One in whom we believe."

I am pleased to report that while my faith was personal, it was definite and determined. I believed for my son, and did not need anyone else to believe for me. I directly spoke to Jesus and simply accepted His declaration that my son would not die. I was not playing a charade. My faith went beyond curiosity. So I did not need to hurry home. I let my faith relax in the miracle worker!

I must admit, however, I did not go to Jesus because I believed Him to be the Messiah. I sought Him because He was a miracle worker. He alone could handle my extreme situation.

Jesus' response to my plea for help was to all the Galilean listeners. Jesus knew they lacked a love for truth. "'Unless you people see miraculous signs and wonders,' Jesus told him, 'you will never believe'" (John 4:48). While it included me, Jesus' statement was to focus attention on His person, not His miracles. He did not seek public attention. All He wanted was, as Leon Morris writes, "for people to trust him and follow him in faith."

Obviously, Jesus knew His power and had a strategy to display it. As Alexander Maclaren explains, "He here puts aside the apparently pressing and urgent necessity in order to deal with a far deeper, more pressing one."

In other words, Jesus wanted me and others to know Him personally as the Son of God and let the signs and wonders come in their time. At that point, I was thinking only of my son. I did not recognize Jesus' divine character. All I knew was that Jesus did not refuse me or my request. Nor did He say I did not have any faith. But, for some strange reason, while He seemed to overlook me, mysteriously He was not denying my petition.

What was Jesus saying? He was saying that, in general, people want to see the spectacular. They do not want to believe He is God's Son. That is, faith based solely on miracles is inauthentic. Besides, as Homer A. Kent, Jr., writes, "... faith based only on seeing miraculous deeds is superficial and requires a succession of miracles to nourish it ...Those who followed Him because of miracles alone soon drifted away."

My faith was so deliberate, I was willing to trust Jesus. So, I insisted that He come to my house to heal my son. Even though I was the boy's father and the king's servant, I was helpless to heal anyone.

I soon discovered that Jesus' power is available to those who ask in faith. And, when He intervenes, it is never too late.

My reply to Jesus was, "Sir, come down before my child dies" (John 4:49). I was impatient and distraught. My son's life was on the edge. I could not depend on religious institutions with their rituals. I would not trust the established church, which is sometimes unconcerned about human need. So, I pressed Jesus to act. He was my only hope.

Jesus would not turn away my call for help. But, by His action, He indicated that His physical presence was not essential for a miracle. His response was, "You may go. Your son will live" (John 4:50). To me, that was more than sympathy. It was empathy filled with a surprise of healing and miraculous grace. Although I thought Jesus should come to my house and see my son, I accepted what He said, believed His Word and headed for home with His promise ringing in my ears.

On my way, my house servants met me with the news that my child was completely cured. When I asked what time it had happened, they said, "The fever left him yesterday at the seventh hour" (John 4:52). That was Roman time, the same time I had spoken to Jesus. As a result, my whole household believed in Him.

In retrospect, what did I have to go on? Nothing — only Jesus' word, *Your son will live.* So, I had to leave His presence just as I had entered it, alone. And, alone, I clung to His promise.

Why did I go to Jesus? Because, as Joseph Parker says, the One who "had turned water into wine was proof enough to the nobleman that he could also turn disease into health." In fact, His healing power could touch every point on the circle of human need, even the circumference of the whole universe.

2

Deliverance for the Disabled

The Impotent Man
John 5:1-9

It was the Feast of Passover, our grand festival. All Jews were celebrating our deliverance from Egyptian bondage. According to John Phillips, "The Jews believed that on this day the Lord gave the law to Moses, on this day He created the world."

But, I was not in any mood to celebrate. I was an invalid, a paralytic, a crippled man for thirty-eight years. I was interested more in my own deliverance at the pool of healing waters. However, the loss of nerve action in my legs *froze* my muscles as stiff as a board, rendering them numb and useless. I could not roll my crippled body to the water's edge.

Thirty-eight years is a long time to live with the same affliction. At times, I had given up any hope of recovery. I often succumbed to doubt and self-pity. Society had banned me. The synagogue's visitation committee didn't bother to visit. It was out of sight, out of mind.

That's the nature of sickness and disease. They are everywhere. Perfect health is hardly a reality anymore. Sin and disease find ways to whip a man to his grave. Health is a mystery, not disease. And, when it comes to God's part in it all, "It is a dreadful thing to fall into the hands of the living God" (Heb. 10:31). Who can deliver himself from God's hand?

For some, the world has become a hospital, for others, an asylum. We do not know who is suffering, because most sick people are not in hospitals.

Our world is a huge pool surrounded by all kinds of hurting people. They are abused, crippled, helpless, homeless, lonely and unsuccessful. However, we all had the same wish, to get well. But we all needed help. We were weak and helpless. In fact, our helplessness was so common that any would-be helpers simply overlooked us. I know people became careless about me and I became hopeless about myself.

My little world of beggars congregated at the sheep market to ask for alms. Then we would struggle and jostle to the nearby pool of Bethesda to wait for the moving of the waters. It was quite a busy place. Farmers would direct their flocks through the Sheep Gate to be sacrificed in the Temple while the afflicted would shuffle for a spot near the pool. The word *Bethesda* means *house of mercy*. Consequently, it generated a wealth of excitement, especially because we were not required to pay for God's free mercy.

Some believed the pool at Bethesda was mineral water which had healing properties. This was pure superstition, but to try their *luck*, people with various diseases came to get into the water.

John Phillips reports: "Some who have visited the area have described the waters as having a reddish color, probably from deposits of iron or other chemicals. The pool had the kind of reputation associated nowadays with a healing spa."

As you may have heard, the pool was deep in the ground. I would have to descend several steps to get to the water. In fact, I had been to this pool before and often seen the *troubled* waters. But, as I slowly struggled to even touch the water, someone else would beat me to it.

8

Bethesda had five covered colonnades or sheltered porches. Actually, Bethesda was the upper fountain of Siloam, and called the Fountain of the Virgin. Invalids like me used the porches while waiting to get into the agitated waters.

Those porches were once used by the rich for self-indulgent pleasure. Over time, they became hospitals, accommodating people who lost their health or limbs and suffered pain and sorrow. There wasn't a healthy person among us; some were blind, crippled or diseased.

We were victims of various diseases and expressed ourselves with moans, groans, cries and prayers, all waiting for relief from the churning waters. We were all in some kind of pain and could not get used to it. But, we could get used to the sin that caused it. Strange, isn't it?

According to some, the pool had a secret. That is, occasionally, the water became agitated or troubled. It churned and surged as if by an undercurrent. It was so mysterious that some folk believed an angel stirred it, giving it creative power.

In J. Rendel Harris' research, he "found evidence in several places throughout the East of a superstition to the effect that at the New Year an angel was expected to stir the water in certain localities, enabling one person to obtain healing by being the first to get into the water after the disturbance. On this basis he judged the feast of this chapter to have been Trumpets, announcing the New Year." Everett F. Harrison reports, "The remains of the Church of St. Anne include the figure of an angel, testifying to this belief and the custom of seeking healing under these special conditions."

However, according to Leon Morris, "Nowhere in Scripture do we have anything like an angel's coming and doing works of healing on a haphazard basis."

Ideally, the best time for a dip and a cure was when the water was stirred. Some of the sick people could enter on their own steam. Others, however, had to depend on family and friends to assist them.

I was one who needed help. After thirty-eight years, my condition had worsened. I had lost weight, and was mentally discouraged. But, day by day, I dragged my paralyzed limbs to the healing water. The priority of my life was the desire for wholeness. I had a fixed purpose to be healed. But, I could not help myself. I needed someone to literally throw me into the water. The situation indicates "the hasty movement required to bring him to the water before its agitation should have ceased."

Although I had been to the pool before, the water did not help me at all. To me, as Simon J. Kistemaker writes, "Bethesda was not so much a house of mercy as a house of misery."

There I was, a human being with potential, dragging myself to a popular pool of plight, yet bubbling with many prospects. However, I was reduced to helplessness. A man without a friend. I was alone.

Then, something wonderful, yet unexpected, happened. Being a cripple, I could not go to Jesus, so He came to me. This is the approach of God in salvation, and often His approach to healing. As one of your gospel songs describes, "Then I Met the Master," and my life changed for the better.

This stranger was Jesus, the Miracle Worker from Nazareth. He was in Jerusalem for the Feast of Passover, and learned that I had been lame for thirty-eight years. He asked, "Do you want to get well?" (John 5:6). I told him I did, but I needed help to get into the pool while the water was stirred. I was too slow and others were getting the blessing ahead of me. The best I could do was limp as near to the pool as possible, expecting my years of infirmity to end in deliverance.

By His question, Jesus was saying He knew I wanted to get well. After all, that's why I was there. John Phillips explains, "Divine omnipotence never violates the sanctity of the will. God does not ravish; he woos. The Lord will neither heal nor save people against their will." Obviously, as Jesus knew Nathanael and the Samaritan woman, He knew my affairs as well.

To me, Jesus' question was my wake-up call. I had settled into a pattern. I was a beggar. If I was delivered, I would have to take responsibility and get back into the workforce. Did I really want to get better?

William Barclay explains it like this: "The first essential towards receiving the power of Jesus is the intense desire for it. Jesus comes to us and says: 'Do you really want to be changed?' If in our inmost hearts we are well content to stay as we are there can be no change for us. The desire for better things must be surging in our hearts."

To some, thirty-eight years is significant. Leon Morris tells us: "they point out that it was the length of time the Israelites wandered in the wilderness after their disobedience of God (Deut. 2:14). They see in this account a picture of the Jews paralyzed because of their lack of faith, and of Jesus giving healing to those who believed."

The stranger commanded me, "Get up! Pick up your mat and walk." That was a triple order. To get up was one thing, to pick up my bed was another, but to walk was impossible. He wanted me to act, to move and show the power of my healing.

I did not question why I had to carry my bed. And, I did not want to make a shrine out of that place of healing. So, I burned all my bridges of thirty-eight years and triumphantly carried my bed for all to see. In fact, I headed for the Temple, from which I had been excluded during my illness. I wanted to give God thanks for my deliverance and restoration. I was home.

Instantly, I felt power like an electric shock surge through me. So, in a movement of confidence, and very deliberately, I sat up, grabbed my mat and walked away. And this stranger, now my Healer, had disappeared into the crowd. But the atmosphere of His presence still surrounded me. My impotence had met omnipotence.

How did it happen? It was simple, really. At such an encouraging command for me to get up, I realized it was His will to heal me. So, I decided I would trust and obey. Consequently, when my will agreed with His, spiritual electricity produced a current of healing power I could neither resist nor control. Whereas I had limped in, I now leaped out.

The command to pick up my bed was one of omnipotence, and Jesus' commands are His enablings. So, the power by which I arose was not my own.

Next, Jesus ordered me to walk. Herbert Lockyer comments, "There was no provision for a relapse. At the pool with his back on his bed, he now leaves with his bed on his back."

Do you wonder why I had to carry my bedroll? Well, J. Laidlaw suggests, first, to prove I had fully recovered; second, to identify me as the man who had once lain helpless by the pool; and third, to show my faith and appreciation to my Healer.

That's when things got ugly, not so much for me, but for Jesus. The problem was, the Pharisees accused me of carrying my bed on the Sabbath. Instead of rejoicing over my deliverance, those Sanhedrins charged me with breaking the Law. They explained, "It is the Sabbath; the law forbids you to carry your mat" (John 5:10). Here I had an opportunity to make a new start, yet those *spiritual* leaders were more concerned about a broken tradition than a healed man. In the words of Edgar C. James, "They rejected a point of grace in favor of a point of law."

Immediately, those religious leaders wanted to know who had told me to carry my bed. At that time, I did not know Him. Besides, He had disappeared and was lost in the crowd.

Legally speaking, it was lawful to heal on the Sabbath, but unlawful to carry a burden (Ex. 27:21). However, according to R. C. Trench, it was lawful "to do whatever was immediately involved in, and directly followed on, the healing." So, which specific law do they have in mind? *The NIV Study Bible* explains, "It was not the law of Moses but their traditional interpretation of it that prohibited carrying loads of any kind on the Sabbath." Consequently, Pharisaical laws were so confusing and contentious, Jesus proclaimed Himself Lord of the Sabbath. And, it was Jesus who told me to carry my bed.

The religious leaders were always using their authority to oppose the works of Jesus. When they questioned me about my healing, they believed my cure was permanent and I would never be an invalid again. However, my healing aside, their main objection was that it took place on the Sabbath, a holy day.

Really, as G. Campbell Morgan writes, "God has no Sabbath, nor can have while men are lying in this derelict condition." God had rested, but when man sinned, His rest was broken; and He has been restless ever since, saving, healing and maintaining the universe.

The fact is, Jesus healed six others on the Sabbath, the man born blind (John 9:1-14), the demoniac in Capernaum (Mark 1:21-27), Peter's mother-in-law (Mark 1:29-31), the man with the withered hand (Mark 3:1-6), the bent-over woman (Luke 13:10-17), and the man with dropsy (Luke 14:1-6).

Returning to the Temple, I encountered Jesus again. In fact, speaking as God in His own name and with authority, He approached me saying, "See, you are well again. Stop sinning or something worse may happen to you" (John 5:14). By telling me to stop sinning, Jesus was showing the connection between my moral life and my physical life. After all, where the spiritual is wrong, the physical is wrong. At the same time, Jesus expressed perfect knowledge in that He knew my past sin and what could happen in the future. However, I took it as a challenge to use my new physical life to start a new spiritual life.

I am ashamed to admit that my physical disability was the result of a moral sin of the flesh. That was not the case with every sick person, nor is it the case today. However, Scripture seems to indicate that sin and sickness can be related (James 5:16-18).

With reference to sickness and sin, F. F. Bruce says that "Jesus was far from thinking that sickness and suffering were necessarily the result of one's sin ... [but] he knew what the cause of his infirmity was, and let him know that He knew."

Augustine comments that those strict Jews "sought darkness from the Sabbath more than light from the miracle." To them, breaking the Sabbath meant loosening all its parts, with the intent of destroying the entire Sabbatical institution.

In explaining why He healed on the Sabbath, Jesus said, "My Father is always at his work to this very day, and I, too, am working" (John 5:17). By referring to God as "My Father," Jesus was showing a closeness to Him that the Jews did not have. They might say "Father," but never "*My* Father." While God rested after finishing creation (Gen. 2:2-3), He has not rested from everything. Consequently, He sustains "all things by his powerful word" (Heb. 1:3). So, on the basis of being equal with God,

Jesus continues to do what His Father would do, especially healing bodies and forgiving sinners.

Are you wondering if Jesus healed others besides me? Well, I do not know. After all, several were afflicted worse than I. As I understand it, it was not in God's sovereign purpose to heal others at that time.

I know also that certain people are so used to their afflictions and dead-end situations, they give up expecting any recovery.

Jesus evidently had a double purpose in healing me, first, to show His deity and equality with His Father; second, to destroy misleading ideas about the Sabbath.

But why was I so blessed? Perhaps so I would have compassion on others. However, I had to be careful because blessings often make us selfish and impatient with other sufferers. The truth is, in the words of Joseph Parker, "a man has not undergone Christian healing if he has no care about healing others."

In a sense, my healing cost Jesus His life. How so? Well, because Jesus healed me on the Sabbath and told me to carry my bed. This action so stirred Jewish anger against Him, they tried to find Him to kill Him. Not only were they opposed to Jesus healing me, they criticized Him for breaking the Sabbath and calling God His Father.

Have you ever passed by the *pool* surrounded by hurting people? Do you sometimes contribute to their charity and go on your way to feasting and entertainment? Do you feel guilty because you cannot say, "Get up! Pick up your mat and walk"?

3

Deliverance for the Demoniac

The Possessed Man
Mark 1:21-28

According to Christian author, Tim Stafford, "Nowhere in the Bible does Jesus or anyone else give lessons in how to heal or cast out demons. Many students of the Bible have poured over it, trying to learn from what Jesus did, but they don't discover an operating manual, or even any standard practices. Sometimes Jesus laid hands on people, sometimes he rubbed mud on them, sometimes he healed from across town. Sometimes he gave orders verbally to a disease or a demon; sometimes he declared healing to the person in need; sometimes he prayed, and other times he did not."

Jesus and four of His followers, Peter, Andrew, James and John, visited Capernaum. On the Sabbath, they worshipped in the local synagogue where Jesus preached. His congregation appreciated His teaching, especially because His authority was superior to that of the scribes, the teachers of the Law. His sermon was based on the Scriptures, not the opinions of men.

According to David L. McKenna, Jesus' authority was not an "inherited authority," like that of a king born into a royal line. Neither did He exercise "delegated authority," such as that given to the president of a corporation. Nor did He have an "achieved authority" based upon academic preparation, research and experience. Instead, Jesus had "inherent authority" and could lay claim to be the Christ, the Son of God.

At Capernaum, the emblem over the synagogue's doorway read, "The seven-branched candlestick," signifying that the building was to be used for illumination and instruction in the Law. In fact, from the time Ezra and Nehemiah established synagogues, the Jews used the synagogue for Sabbath worship. During the week, it was used for instruction, discussion and administration of justice. Often, synagogue leaders discussed the problem of demons.

When first created, angels were messengers of God, without sin. But, one-third revolted against God, submitted to Satan and sought acceptance with humans. In time, one entered my body, shrunk my self-worth, twisted my personality and manipulated my speech. As Herbert Lockyer points out, "What the Devil cannot keep as his own, he will, if he can, destroy."

Apparently, Jesus' sermon exposed the demons as to who they were and their whereabouts. They knew all about Jesus and His power to destroy them. However, they wanted more time to destroy me before Jesus destroyed them. Actually, they were saying that Jesus was not finished with them yet.

I had the demon; rather, the demon had me. That is, an evil or unclean spirit gripped and controlled me, giving me erratic speech and unmanageable actions. This spirit was trying to stop me from worshipping God, although I was not barred from public worship.

Not only that, but the demon was intent on destroying me. As members of Satan's kingdom, demons hate those created in the image of God. William Barclay quotes Adolf von Harnack: "The whole world ... [was] filled with devils; not merely idolatry, but every phase and form of life was ruled by them. They sat on thrones, they hovered around cradles. The earth was literally a hell."

I was not controlled 24/7; otherwise, I would not be allowed in the synagogue. But, I had occasions of possession. During those times, I lusted and acted abnormally. I pondered impure thoughts and they seized me. I became a conduit for anger and verbal abuse beyond my control. I was under the dominion of a spirit which tyrannized me with fear and deprived me of freedom and normal family life. Actually, it kept me in spiritual bondage and tried to be my god.

Such demons could cause mental disorder (John 10:20), violent action (Luke 8:26-29), bodily disease (Luke 13:11, 16) and rebellion against God (Rev. 16:14).

The demon was part of a team in the work of evil. Speaking as one voice, it suddenly interrupted the sermon by shouting, "What do you want with us, Jesus of Nazareth? Have you come to destroy us? I know who you are – the Holy One of God!"

Then, silence. Not that it was rare in synagogues, but this was different. It was the kind you could cut with a knife. You could hear a pin drop. That spirit belonged to a kingdom totally different from the kingdom of God. Yet, the spirit, showing superior knowledge, affirmed Jesus to be the "Holy One of God," God's divine Son.

The fact is, the demon knew Jesus to be without sin, equal with His Father and set apart or anointed to be the Messiah. So, using Jesus' name gave the demon a perceived control over Jesus. But, in reality, a demon knows when its death knell has sounded.

All demons recognize Jesus to be the Holy One, sent to destroy all persons and powers of ungodliness in the realm of Satan's operation. And, for certain, they perceived Jesus to be the woman's seed that would bruise Satan's head and destroy all his works (Gen. 3:15). For Christ to triumph over demons was the heart of His ministry. In fact, if *one* is punished, *all* would be punished.

Jesus was a regular teacher in our synagogue. While I listened to His sermon, the demon inside me recognized Jesus. Its plan was to disturb the preacher and divert a receptive audience. In this way, Jesus' Word would be unfruitful and unprofitable.

I must say, Jesus' teaching was not the type to which we were accustomed. It was not a droning of weary words and ritualistic obedience. Alexander Maclaren observes that this new Teacher was like "an eagle suddenly appearing in a Sanhedrin of owls." He did not quote anyone, not even Moses. He did not have to say, "Thus saith the Lord." He did not argue, but declared the truth because He is the Truth.

Really, the demon's question was, "What do we have in common?" The answer is, Jesus came into the world to destroy the evil practices of the demon, who knew he had a date with destiny.

Jesus sternly replied, "Be quiet! Come out of him!" That was a call for instant obedience and a command not to reveal Jesus' identity.

There I was, caught between the demon and Jesus. The demon wanted to get His attention; it did not want me to get Jesus' attention. But, with authoritative words and actions, Jesus quelled all input from the demonic world.

Jesus' rebuke is the only sovereign power to which Satan yields. So, the muzzled demon's options were to send me into convulsions, make me scream with anger or abandon me on the spot. So, the demon opted to leave; and I was free.

Haldor Lillenas (1885-1959) and Alfred Judson expressed it in their song, *Glorious Freedom*.

Once I was bound by sin's galling fetters;
Chained like a slave, I struggled in vain.
But I received a glorious freedom
When Jesus broke my fetters in twain.

CHORUS
Glorious freedom! Wonderful freedom!
No more in chains of sin I repine!
Jesus the glorious Emancipator!
Now and forever He shall be mine.

Freedom from fear and all of its torments;
Freedom from care with all of its pain;
Freedom in Christ, my blessed Redeemer,
He who has rent my fetters in twain.

According to William U. Taylor, the unclean and impure demon "violently recoiled from the unsullied holiness which dwelt in Christ ... and was unable to endure it, so he cried out in fear." The truth is, as Joseph Parker writes, "Wickedness [is] always afraid of purity." It is never friendly to personal rights, safety and the enrichment of humanity. It has no truth, reason and hope.

"The concentrated demonic attack during Jesus' ministry was part of Satan's attack on the kingdom. Moreover, it was the work of Jesus to expose the spiritual corruption of the world, and to bring to light the demonic influences prevalent among the people. It was the work of Jesus to deliver a death-blow to Satan and his legions. Thus, Jesus declared holy war on the realm of unclean spirits."

Again, the people were amazed at Jesus' powerful miracle. It was a vivid demonstration of His authority and power. Without orchestrated techniques and emotional gymnastics, He spoke the Word only and the unclean spirits obeyed Him. In my mind, Jesus did not depend on the traditions of earlier generations. His teaching was not empty. He made things happen.

My deliverance had far-reaching, positive effects. The people who witnessed my miracle were shocked and surprised. They asked each other if it was a new teaching and what it meant. They admitted that evil spirits obeyed Him. And, Jesus' reputation rose significantly. People declared Him to be a Teacher from God. In fact, this was the first time they saw teaching supported by a miracle.

Obviously, one cannot resist Jesus' authority. Demons cannot ignore His voice, nor escape His power. Now, since His resurrection and ascension, "all angels, authorities, and powers are subject to Him," according to Simon J. Kistemaker.

Are there still demons in the synagogue? Yes. Herbert Lockyer concludes: "When, in buildings erected for the preaching of the inspired, infallible Scriptures, preachers discredit the reliability of the Bible, repudiate the miracles, flout the virgin birth, the atoning blood, and the physical resurrection of Christ, what are they with all their education and polish but demons in the synagogue? As they do not represent the Spirit of truth, some other spirit must possess them. We are enjoined to have no fellowship with such unfruitful works of darkness, but rather reprove them (Eph. 5:11)."

4

Deliverance from Distress

Peter's Mother-in-law
Mark 1:29-31

I suspect most of us are familiar with fevers. Fever, pyrexia or controlled hyperthermia is when our body's temperature goes above the normal range of 36-37 degrees C or 98-100 degrees F. According to most family doctors, a rising body temperature is one way our immune system tries to combat infection. However, our temperature may rise too high, resulting in serious complications.

Mothers-in-law are typically the victims of bad jokes. But not in my case. I must say, Peter, my son-in-law, usually spoke well of me.

Incidentally, Peter's marriage to my daughter did not make the marriage a virtue. Although marriage is a divine institution, it is no guarantee against failure. At the same time, Peter was not controlled by what Herbert Lockyer calls "enforced celibacy."

My story of deliverance occurred on the Sabbath in the synagogue. While preaching on the Old Testament Scriptures, Jesus expelled a demon from a man. Afterwards, He took James and John to Peter and Andrew's house for the Sabbath meal. Since my husband was dead, I lived with my daughter and Peter (1 Cor. 9:5). During their visit, I had a high fever and remained in bed.

Some believe I had typhus which developed into typhoid fever. Typhus is an acute infectious disease marked by fever, headache and skin rash, and transmitted by fleas, lice, etc. Full-blown typhoid attacks the intestines and is acquired from contaminated food or water.

According to Dr. Luke, I was seriously ill and could die (Luke 4:38). William L. Lane explains that "in the ancient world fever was regarded as an independent disease and not as a distress accompanying a variety of illnesses."

When they told Jesus of my condition, He took my hand and helped me up. The fever immediately left me and I proceeded to tend on them. Consequently, after sunset, when people were free to travel at least two-thirds of a mile, many brought their sick to Peter's house. It seems like everyone in Capernaum showed up.

Jesus knew my problem and overpowered the fever. He did not associate it with sin, nor did He take an X-ray. But, with tender-loving care, He touched me and the fever left (Matt. 8:15). Herbert Lockyer says, "Through His hand there flowed that supernatural energy producing a direct and immediate cure."

According to Mark, Jesus' life-giving touch brought health and strength to my weak frame. My healing was instant. And, I used my recovery to prepare and serve the Sabbath meal. After all, as Frederick Dale Bruner reports, "it was not [my] service that released Jesus' grace; it was his grace that released [my] service."

William Barclay explains: "According to Jewish custom the main Sabbath meal came immediately after the synagogue service, at the sixth hour, that is at 12 o'clock midday. (The Jewish day began at 6 a.m. and the hours are counted from then.)"

To take someone by the hand was customary for Jesus. Alexander Maclaren says, "His grasp means sympathy, tenderness, identification of Himself with us, the communication of upholding, restoring strength." And, happily for them, Jesus healed many and drove out numerous demons. But, Jesus would not let the demons speak because they could identify Him.

Surprisingly, Jesus took time to cure women. After all, in my day, women were like used property, ignored as inferior beings. In the synagogue, we were screened off at the back. However, Jesus considered me and my need, not the least of all women, but a man's mother-in-law.

The point is, Jesus did not embarrass me. He used His "unique knowledge together with unique power" to expel my fever. In fact, Luke 4:39 says Jesus rebuked my fever "as if addressing the outbreak of some hostile power." And, He would not tolerate any resistance.

When the news of my healing got out, it caused quite a stir, awakening hope in other sufferers. Matthew 8:17 says my healing and that of others fulfilled what Isaiah prophesied: "He took up our infirmities and carried our diseases" (Isa. 53:4). That is, Christ not only died for our sin, but also provided healing for our bodies.

What does my healing illustrate? It typifies Israel's restoration. Just as Jesus touched my hand, so He will touch the nation of Israel and restore it to full health.

My deliverance displays Jesus' sensitivity to human need. Consequently, He will not forget His covenants with the Hebrew people (Matt. 8:26-36). At the same time, He will remain faithful to us and secure Israel's future (Ezek. 37:11-14).

My miracle of healing was not to prove or strengthen Christ's mission, but simply to demonstrate His love to me and to Israel. In my case, as Alexander Maclaren indicates, Jesus "responded to the sight of human sorrow."

Incidentally, I did not pray for my healing. And, Jesus did not ask me if I believed He could heal me. But, my healing tells us something about

Him. He could use His healing power in a private home or in a public synagogue. He was never too tired to help, but showed interest in, and gave priority to, the needs of others. And, He never relied on spells, magic or incantations, but with a word or a touch, the work was done. For me, as R. Kent Hughes writes, it was Jesus' "sympathetic love" which reached out to me with deliverance.

Edith G. Cherry describes my healing in her poem, *The Master's Touch*.

He touched her hand, and the fever left her,
He touched her hand as He only can,
With the wondrous skill of the Great Physician,
With tender touch of the Son of Man.
And the eyes, where the fever light had faded.
Looked up, by her grateful tears made dim;
She rose and ministered to her household,
She rose and ministered unto Him.

And many a life is one long fever –
The fever of anxious suspense and care,
The fever of fretting, the fever of getting,
The fever of hurrying here and there.

He touched her hand and the fever left her,
Oh, blessed touch of the Man Divine!
How beautiful then to arise and serve Him
When the fever is gone from your life and mine.

And someday, after life's fitful fever,
Methinks we shall say in the home on high:
"If the hands that He touched but did His bidding,
How little it matters what else went by."

Ah! Lord, Thou knowest us altogether,
Each heart's sore sickness, whate'er it be,
Touch Thou our hands, let the fever leave us,
And so shall we minister unto Thee.

5

Deliverance for the Detached

The Leper
Mark 1:40-45

I don't have a name, at least not in public. I am known as *a man with leprosy*. Consequently, in our group of lepers, we were ceremonially unclean, outcasts of society (Lev. 13:11). It was the worst disease during the days of Jesus. Today, it is called Hansen's disease.

Herbert Lockyer writes: "The Jews called leprosy 'the finger of God,' or 'the stroke,' indicating thereby that the disease was regarded as a direct punishment from God and absolutely incurable, except by the same divine power which permitted it." Most people considered leprosy as "the dirty sign of God's damnation," to quote David A. Redding.

When my leprosy reached its climax, I was disfigured and banned from the community. Since the Law could not cure us, it did something to protect the community – it drove all of us out of town, to create our own colony.

Our colony was strictly for lepers. Some of us were *nodular* lepers, that is, having leprosy in our back, face and joints, for up to nine years. Pink and brown nodules, or small rounded lumps, would appear in our nose, lips and forehead, and the folds of our cheeks. Eventually, our skin would turn white. Then, those nodules would break, producing a foul discharge. Our hands and feet would be affected, our voices would become hoarse and our eyebrows would fall off. Others in our colony were *anaesthetic* lepers, that is, having our nerve trunks affected. We were unaware of losing all sensation. We could not sense pain from burns and scalds. Our muscles became like jelly. And, our hands and feet turned into claws, before they finally dropped off.

Most lepers in a colony are a mixture of nodular and anaesthetic. The disease includes ringworm and psoriasis, with white scales covering the body. In this condition, I was forced to wear torn clothes, shave my head and call "unclean" to warn the unsuspecting public of what George B. Telford Jr. calls my "polluted presence."

Lepers lived hopeless lives because the disease was incurable. I was a walking sepulchre. In your day, lepers can be treated with antibiotics. But in my day, to quote Simon J. Kistemaker, "those parts of the body that have been affected can never be restored."

This is a picture of spiritual leprosy. The Apostle Paul declares, "for all have sinned and fall short of the glory of God" (Rom. 3:23). The trouble is, like all diseased lepers, we are insensitive to our sin. We are dead *in* sin and *to* sin. Only God's Word can give us faith to believe and to convince us of our sin (Rom. 10:17; John 16:8-11).

That was me. I knew my spiritual and physical condition, but I was willing to trust Jesus to touch me and make me clean.

William L. Lane explains that, in certain places, "Lepers were allowed to live unhampered wherever they chose, except in Jerusalem and cities which had been walled from antiquity. They could even attend the synagogue services if a screen was provided to isolate them from the rest of the congregation." When news of a coming miracle worker reached our colony of huts, it ignited sparks of hope in every heart. One of us, some of us, maybe all of us would be delivered. That would be awesome!

Following Jesus' Sermon on the Mount, the thought of healing gave me hope and courage. Besides, I wanted to worship and reverence Him. After all, I called Him "Lord" because He was superior to me (Matt. 8:2). So, in my determination, I wormed my way forward and fell on my knees at Jesus' feet. I wanted Him to remove what William Lane calls "the ravages and stigma of this dreadful disease." I simply stated. "If you are willing, you can make me clean."

I could tell that Jesus had compassion on my desperate situation because He reached out and touched me, declaring, "I am willing. Be clean!"

When Jesus reached His hand toward me, I knew He was unafraid of becoming unclean. Rather, His compassion was superior to the Law's ritual and ceremony. So, when Jesus sent out the Twelve, He commanded them to "cleanse those who have leprosy" (Matt. 10:8).

R. Kent Hughes describes Jesus' compassion as going "beyond pity and sympathy or even empathy." David L. McKenna elaborates, "Not just mind for mind, hand for hand, or even heart for heart, but stomach for stomach, blood for blood, gut for gut, Jesus feels His way into the leper's needs."

Alexander Maclaren points out: "All true sympathy involves a touch. Jesus reaches the leper with the touch of a universal love and pity which disregards all that is repellent and overflows every barrier. He is high above us and yet bending over us. He stretches his hand from the throne as truly as he put it out when here on earth. And he is ready to take us all to his heart – in spite of our weakness and shortcomings ... This Christ lays hold on us because he loves us, and will not be turned from his compassion by our most loathsome foulness." All things considered, I was healed immediately.

The highlight of my story was when Jesus connected with me by His touch. Brooke Foss Westcott says the word *touch* "expresses more than superficial contact." It is often translated *to take hold of.* When Jesus put His hand firmly on me, and His pure fingers touched my rotting ulcers, ecstasy surged through me, shocking the onlookers and amazing the disciples. Yet Jesus didn't even become ceremonially unclean.

Why not? Because He is God. Herbert Lockyer explains, "The sun shines on earth's pollution but remains unscathed in its own purity and splendour." Consequently, "God made him who had no sin to be sin for us, so that in him we might become the righteousness of God" (2 Cor. 5:21).

Following my healing, Jesus sent me away with a triple warning: don't mention this to anybody, report your healing to your priest, and give an offering for your cleansing.

Why did Jesus tell me to keep quiet about my healing? Because, according to Donald W. Burdick, "Until pronounced clean by the authorities, he had no right to resume his normal social relationships." Besides, publicity would divert focus away from Jesus' message. He did not want to be known only as a miracle worker. And, He did not want to die before finishing His local ministry.

Along with Jesus' compassion, I detected His righteous indignation against what William Lane calls "sin, disease and death which take their toll even upon the living, a toll particularly evident in a leper." I knew He was willing and I had not asked in vain.

Oddly enough, true compassion has an element of anger in it. In Jesus' case, He was angry when He saw how evil manifested itself in my body and He longed to do something to help me and to settle my doubts.

Besides, I did not want to interrupt Jesus' preaching mission, because He had a heart to reach out to the next towns.

But, why report to my priest? Because the priest must verify my healing (Lev. 13:1-46). And, Jesus respected the Law. He knew the Jewish belief was that only God could cure leprosy.

Why should I make an offering for my cleansing? Because I must follow the Old Testament's regulations for proper reinstatement into society. In fact, I would remain ceremonially unclean until I had paid an offering of two birds, one sacrificed and one set free (Lev. 14:1-32). Only then could the priest publicly confirm my healing. Jesus wanted my healing to be a testimony to God's power. In other words, I would be a witness or proof to the priests so they could confirm my miracle. That is, the *defence* would win in spite of the *prosecution*.

In addition, Jesus knew I should control my highest moments of inspiration, at least until I had seen the priest. I should regulate my ecstasy so as not to endanger the real purpose of my healing – to bring glory to God.

Myra Brooks' classic poem, *The Touch of the Master's Hand*, expresses my sentiments — only the Master's touch can restore the human soul to its original value.

6

Deliverance by Detour

The Paralytic on the Roof
Mark 2:3-12

A few days after Jesus healed the leper (Mark 1:40-45) and completed His tour of Galilee, He returned to Capernaum, His own town. News quickly spread that He was at the house which probably belonged to Peter (Matt. 4:13).

Bethlehem was Jesus' birthplace and Nazareth was where He grew up; but Capernaum was His residence during His ministry.

Most Capernaum houses measured about 9 x 10 or 12 x 15 feet, were made of stone and belonged to poor people. Outside, stone stairs led to a roof constructed of branches, straw and clay laid on wooden rafters. St. Luke describes what Merrill C. Tenney refers to as "the house as a Roman dwelling with a tile roof."

A standing-room-only crowd blocked the entrance of the humble home to hear Jesus' teaching. They heard about life and how it should be lived. In fact, as David A. Redding writes, "Men came because Jesus had the answers to the very things that were killing them." In reality, they wanted something more exciting than teaching.

In the crowd were four specific men carrying a stretcher or mattress bed. I was on that bed, suffering from severe paralysis. I was a quadriplegic. Those men wanted to help me, even going beyond the call of duty. The word *can't* was not in their vocabulary. *We must* was their motto. Difficulties tested, challenged and increased their faith.

Still holding the mattress, they started reducing the distance between Jesus and me. They reasoned that if I was to walk again, they had to get me into the arms of compassion. But, they ran into an obstacle. The large crowd blocked the door to the house. My four friends could not get me to Jesus. So, not letting such a small problem stop them, they carried me upstairs to the roof. Then, stretching their backs and wiping the sweat from their brows, they quickly removed the tile and lowered me down right in front of Jesus.

This action of my friends was an expression of their faith and mine. Obviously, they knew that "faith without deeds is useless" (James 2:20). For them, Jesus was my only hope. They would face all obstacles to get me to Him. As Richard Chenevix Trench points out, their faith was "a faith which overcame hindrances, and was not to be baffled by difficulties." It was not a fragile faith looking for an excuse to give up. No, this quartet of faith determined to get through to Jesus. Then, laughing at impossibilities, they made an opening that doubters never thought was there. Sceptics would have said, "Come in through the door like the rest of us." But, penetrating all barriers, they chose to be different, regardless of the cost.

When Jesus told me to "Take heart, son" (Matt. 9:2), He was admonishing me to take courage. He used the Greek word *tharseo*, meaning "There is nothing to be afraid of." So, while the palsy shook me uncontrollably, my friends lowered my disabled body through the roof until I came to rest in front of Jesus.

I appreciate friends like that. I identify them as Faith, Consecration, Compassion and Intercession. They are necessary to turn despair into hope.

An issue of *Our Daily Bread* carries the following story:

"A young man who was rebelling against God took a trip to the West Coast. He arrived in San Francisco, restless and irritable. Soon he had spent all his money drinking and carousing.

"After a night of revelry, he staggered to his hotel room in the wee hours of the morning and fell asleep. When he awoke, he saw a small book on a bedside table. It was the Gospel of Mark. Disgusted, he flung it to the floor.

"That evening when he returned, he saw that the book had been placed back on the night stand. Again he brushed it aside. But the next day when he saw it there, he opened it and began to read. When he finished reading it, he was a changed man. In his own words, here's what happened: 'I learned that the Son of God said to a leper, "Be cleansed." He said to a paralyzed man, "Your sins are forgiven you." I was impressed when Jesus took little children in His arms and blessed them. And then, in spite of the unjust way He was treated, He shed His blood to save sinners. When I read that, I saw my own guilt and found peace in believing.'"

In my day, the Jews generally believed that all sickness resulted from personal sin. However, Jesus declared my sins forgiven, dismissed and driven away. I was now free from my sins and guilt.

The fact is, only the one sinned against has the option to forgive. So, when Jesus forgives, it is necessary and complete. As I understand it, that's the essence of the gospel. John S. Whale declares that Christianity's distinctive is the forgiveness of sins.

The scribes, the teachers of the Law, were sitting there with furrowed brows and glaring eyes, taking it all in. After all, they studied and taught the Law, and were allies of the Pharisees. They had to make sure that everything was done *by the book*. That is, they wanted to know that Jesus' "teaching was mainstream doctrine in harmony with theirs." Consequently, they objected to the whole thing, accusing Jesus of acting like God, which is blasphemy. And, they were right in saying that only God can forgive sins.

But, they were wrong by refusing to see Jesus as God. Jesus' direct action showed His claim to deity.

Did the hole in the roof disturb Jesus? Did He accuse the Devil of interrupting His teaching? Not at all. In fact, He used the incident to forgive and heal. Besides, maybe His Father thought the meeting needed improvement.

In His spirit, Jesus knew what the scribes were thinking and asked them, "Why are you thinking these things?" To help them understand, He then asked, "Which is easier: to say to the paralytic, 'Your sins are forgiven,' or to say, 'Get up, take your mat and walk'?" That is, which is easier, forgiveness or healing?

The point is, for man, forgiveness, while difficult, is easier. For God, forgiveness and healing are easy. Only He has divine authority to instantly heal and forgive. In their hymn, *Rock of Ages*, Augustus M. Toplady and Thomas Hastings describe it appropriately:

Rock of Ages, cleft for me,
Let me hide myself in Thee.
Let the water and the blood,
From Thy wounded side which flowed,
Be of sin the double cure,
Save from wrath and make me pure.

For me, my greater need was forgiveness. So, Jesus addressed it first, even though He was there, in Herbert Lockyer's words, to "accomplish any work of healing."

The fact that Jesus healed me verifies His claim to be God. Even the scribes had to admit, "Who can forgive sins but God alone?" When Jesus identified Himself as the "Son of Man," He had double authority – to forgive our sin and heal our sickness.

As the Son of Man, Jesus was associating Himself with the person in Daniel 7:13-14. Daniel saw "one like a son of man, coming with the clouds of heaven" to receive a kingdom. He represents all God's saints who receive a kingdom. This is the same Son of Man Stephen saw while he was being stoned to death (Acts 7:56).

As my Forgiver and Healer, Jesus told me to pick up my mattress bed and go home, which I did most happily. Actually, my bed, which was a sign of my sickness, became the sign of my cure. This all started with Jesus declaring my pardon, the scribes questioning it, Jesus healing me and confirming my pardon, and the crowd recognizing my miracle.

The crowd responded with amazement and gave glory and praise to God, saying, "We have never seen anything like this!"

The obvious conclusion is that, "When determined people come together in prayer and ask God to bless their efforts that affect his church and kingdom, miracles happen."

7

Deliverance for the Deformed

The Withered Hand
Matthew 12:9-14

You don't know me, but you've heard people refer to me as "the man with the withered hand." Today, I'm in the synagogue at Capernaum, where I'm the guinea pig to set a trap for Jesus. The conflict is over the Sabbath, and I'm the "silent participant in the unfolding situation."

According to Luke 22:50, my hand was shrivelled or paralyzed (1 Kings 13:4). It had lost all stability and strength. I could not control it, not even to extend my fingers. It was not a birth defect, but it hindered me from being gainfully employed. If I wanted to be a bricklayer, I needed both hands.

My story is about experience and common sense. The question is whether or not it is scriptural to heal on the Sabbath. But, it was to trick

Jesus. After all, He and the Pharisees knew what the Law said – no work on the Sabbath unless in a life-threatening situation (Deut. 5:12-15; Exod. 20:8-11).

The word *Sabbath* refers to rest and ceasing. That is, we stop *our* work, but not *God's*. We seek to do good every day; if not, we sin (James 4:17).

The Pharisees, however, stuck to ritual, especially their own oral laws. So, whether it was plucking corn or healing, they were not against either if it wasn't on the Sabbath (Deut. 23:25). Simon J. Kistemaker contends that their "stifling legalism ruled the day."

A delegation from the Sanhedrin, the Jewish Council (Matt. 5:21), was there in the front seats of honour. With their cold eyes, they were supposed to examine and scrutinize all teaching in the synagogue, especially that of Jesus. They were there to trap Jesus, not to worship God. Ironically, they knew He could heal, and wanted to make sure they caught Him in the act. They did not know it, but according to Alexander Maclaren, "There is nothing so blind as formal religionism."

My useless hand meant very little to the Pharisees. They had great zeal for the Law, but did not have any compassion for me and my deformed hand. They did not see that their hearts and minds were deformed just as much as my hand.

The nation of Israel was like that – deformed and helpless through disobedience. And, in many cases, churches are deformed, too. They are self-handicapped, serving and worshipping with only one hand.

Ordinarily, I was not allowed in the synagogue and temple. But, to carry out their plot to trap Jesus in a corner, the Pharisees permitted me to stay. And, I was soon to discover, the merciful God who had preserved my feet was able to restore my useless hand.

Jesus did not like any law that was insensitive to human need. In fact, in His Sermon on the Mount, He set Himself over the sixth, seventh and eighth commandments, especially since the Law did not forbid healing on this holy day (Mark 2:27-28). It opposed working, but healing was not work.

Jesus was not adverse to experience and common sense (Luke 14:5). However, certain people valued property over persons. The Torah conflicted with *agape* love. The Jews did not allow the use of medicine on the Sabbath, unless they thought the sick may die before morning. It is in us to care (Prov. 12:10). When Jesus confronted people on their own ground, He reduced them all to silence.

Jesus concludes that it is biblical to do good on the Sabbath. So, He healed me with only one command. He did not even lift a finger. He said that the Sabbath was made for man, to bless him, profit him and train him to serve God freely. He does not want our ritualistic practice to smother our joy, whether in worship or work. After all, one's relationship with God is more important than one's obedience to laws.

Jesus' philosophy is to do good and preserve life. He "refused to observe the traditional rules; he moved in grace toward sick individuals and healed them without regard to the day of the week."

Jesus ordered me, "Stretch out your hand." I stretched it out and it was completely restored, as sound as the other. I did not question Him. In fact, I did not wonder if I could. I knew my hand was lifeless, but I automatically offered it to Jesus. After all, when He commands, He gives power to obey. And, as David L. McKenna writes, "There is no law against obedience." As James, the Lord's brother, observes, "Anyone, then, who knows the good he ought to do and doesn't do it, sins" (James 4:17).

This was my opportunity and I didn't want to mess it up. So, by faith, when I disregarded all impossibilities, Jesus' divine ability met my human disability, and He restored my right hand like new.

When Jesus healed me, the Pharisees were furious. They held a meeting with the Herodians to discuss how best to destroy Jesus.

David L. McKenna concludes: "Think of it. God's specialists in human salvation counselling with Caesar's specialists in human slaughter. Will we ever learn the lesson? Throughout Christian history, we have repeated examples of entangling alliances between the church and the state. Every time it happens, both the church and the state forsake their God-given functions and become tyrants bent on the destruction of both faith and freedom ... Although the alliance may achieve its short-term goals, the long-term truth is that the people of God have sold their souls."

8

Deliverance for a Diplomat

The Centurion's Servant
Luke 7:1-10

Matthew wrote to Israel about being blessed with Abraham, Isaac and Jacob. But, he also warned Israel about putting religious associations in place of personal faith. Luke wrote to Gentiles, encouraging them to suppress their conceit.

While there are reconcilable differences between Matthew and Luke, I will use Luke because he was a physician and researched his stories for accuracy.

After His Sermon on the Mount, Jesus went to Capernaum, His place of residence. There, He encountered a busy seaside city full of people with problems, typical of your own generation.

I lived in Capernaum where I had earned the respect of the whole community. However, my home life was devastated because my choice servant was very sick and near death. Naturally, I was overly concerned because he was extremely valuable to me. I held him in high esteem. This, of course, was contrary to the reputation of most Roman officers in Israel. As a centurion, I had to be a man who could command, be reliable and steady in action. So, I tried to show kindness rather than cruelty.

Herod Antipas was head over Palestine and I was a commander over one hundred of his soldiers. In fact, we were the backbone of the Roman army. We were stationed in Capernaum to keep Roman law and order.

To many, I was considered a sinner, a heathen. In fact, that's all some people ever see. However, Alexander Maclaren concludes that "the Christianity which ignores sin is sure to be impotent, on the other hand the Christianity which sees little but sin is bondage and misery, and is impotent too."

But, when I heard of Jesus, I sent some older, respected Jews to Him to request Him to come and heal my servant. Because of how well I was accepted in Capernaum, those old synagogue leaders wanted to help all they could. So, they were more than willing to obey my request.

Those elders pled with Jesus on behalf of my servant. In fact, they said I was worthy of this because of my contributions to Capernaum. I did not consider myself godly, or even deserving of anything. However, I did not think that religion was a bartering system to buy favour for heaven or earth.

The elders reported to Jesus that I deserved this favour because I loved the Jewish nation and was responsible for building the local synagogue. That was true, but I tried to have an honest heart and the right motive to please God in the best way possible. As the elders confirmed, I loved the Jewish nation. That is, I saw the people as human beings and wished the best for them. To me, they were important and contributed to society. I built the Jews a synagogue. Actually, I was responsible for convincing Rome to build and finance a new synagogue. According to Acts 10:2, I was similar to Cornelius who gave alms to needy Jews.

At the elders' request, Jesus answered the call for help and agreed to come to my house. Before He approached my home, I sent friends to tell Him of my unworthiness to have Him under my roof. Actually, Jews were not allowed to enter a Gentile house.

Because I could not measure up to Jesus' character and reputation, I did not feel adequate enough to go to Jesus. Simon J. Kistemaker explains: "Jewish people felt free to approach Jesus, but Gentiles hesitated because Jews despised them and placed foreigners on the level of dogs. In addition, Jews had an aversion to military people, for they represented the hated Roman government, whose oppression they had to endure."

Since I did not feel worthy to go to Jesus myself, I suggested all He had to do was speak the healing word and my servant would be healed. I believed He could heal at a distance simply by declaring my servant was well.

Jesus did not think my humility was false. In fact, commenting on my humility, Augustine said, "He counted himself unworthy that Christ should enter his doors, he was counted worthy that Christ should enter his heart." That must be true because, as Alexander Maclaren states, "worthiness or unworthiness has nothing to do with Christ's love." And, Ira F. Stanphill says it's Christ's grace which makes us worthy to be receive His love.

I believed in healing by word only because I practiced it with my soldiers. You see, I respect the chain of command. After all, I am a man with authority, something like Jesus. When I order a soldier to go, he goes. When I command a soldier to come, he comes. Or, when I tell my servant to do something, he does it.

So, to me, distance was nothing to Jesus. Herbert Lockyer observes: "His word at a mile's distance could cure as well as His actual presence and touch. His was a grand faith, desiring no visual sign. His spiritual eye could see the invisible and so his heart was fixed, trusting in the Lord." For me, I expressed my faith by my obedience and surrender.

After Jesus heard my logic, He was amazed. He saw my confidence and faith. This was remarkable, especially since I was a Gentile. Jesus had to admit that He had "not found such great faith even in Israel." That is, to Jesus, my faith "outshone anything He had found amongst the Jews."

When my friends returned to the house, my servant was well. He had been healed at a distance and only by Jesus' Word. Dr. Luke says my servant was made whole. That is, he was in sound health. His disease had suddenly departed. In fact, "The healing word had flowed from Jesus as naturally as the perfume from the flowers."

Obviously, since Jesus can heal bodily sickness by His Word, He is able also to heal man's soul.

That's my story of faith, the faith of one outside the Covenant. My faith did not depend on sight, nor the sense of touch. It was a moral quality of the heart, not based on reason, but produced by love.

9

Deliverance from Death

The Widow's Son
Luke 7:11-16

Luke alone records this touching story, showing Jesus' nature and power, even in the face of death.

Describing this resurrection miracle, Simon J. Kistemaker explains that it is "the first miracle of Jesus calling a dead person back to life." Therefore, as David A. Redding comments, "The gospel ... selects no mummies for its miracles."

After healing the centurion's servant at Capernaum, Jesus travelled to Nain, ten miles south east of Nazareth, followed by His disciples and a large crowd. In fact, the whole village had turned out to grieve with me. Although their hearts were warm, I felt as if I were wrapped in a cold wet cloak.

I was mourning for my dead son when Jesus and His followers entered our town through the eastern gates, the boundary of Nain. Because the Jews did not permit the dead to be interred among the living, a few friends carried my only son downhill to the burying place. As a widow, I could not afford paid mourners. So, a sufficient crowd of Galilean mourners followed us to the cemetery outside the city. Traditionally, however, the kings of David's house were buried inside Jerusalem.

My son's funeral had to be held on the day of his death because keeping his body overnight made my house unclean. So, my friends anointed his body and prepared for the funeral. I was devastated. The *pale horse* of death had robbed me of my only support (Rev. 6:8).

Most mothers can relate to a painful childbirth. However, there isn't anything as painful as losing your only son. Herbert Lockyer says, "A Jewish wife felt it a calamity not to have a son, but it was the most terrible calamity when the only son, the stay and hope of the home, was removed by death."

As you may suspect, I asked myself, why is death intruding on the green lawn of such a young life? Is it, as some contend, a direct punishment for sin?

When Jesus saw me leading the funeral procession, He had compassion for me and said, "Don't cry." According to Luke, He always dealt graciously with women, especially those stricken with grief.

Jesus was always moved by human sorrow. His compassion changed people, leaving them in a better situation. It was deeper than human sympathy. He is a God with a heart, not simply to dry my tears, but to remove the occasion for weeping altogether. In fact, His main mission is, as Alexander Maclaren writes, "to stop the triumphant march of death."

Now, for those who trust Him, "The dread of death is gone forever." And, we can look forward to the time when God shall wipe away all tears (Rev. 21:4).

Then, strictly of His own accord, Jesus approached and touched the open coffin. At that point, the procession stopped and, speaking into the regions of the dead, Jesus declared, "Young man, I say to you, get up!" My son, though separated from me, was not destroyed, but heard Jesus' command and responded immediately. Something like a current mother telling her sulking son to get out of bed to catch the school bus. The angel of death had no other choice but to release its grip on my son and allow his deliverance.

Everyone was surprised at Jesus' action, especially when He touched the coffin. Ceremonially, He would be unclean and defiled if He touched the body. However, this did not happen because His power immediately cancelled the presence of death. Being the authority over life and death, and claiming to work by His own power, Jesus authorized my son's resurrection.

At Jesus' word, my son, without the assistance of sorrowing friends, sat up and began to talk. Then, Jesus presented him to me, alive. This was my most wonderful miracle, an unexpected gift of new life, an action of the unconditional grace of God.

The people responded with godly fear and a reverent awe for our life-giving Lord, our divine Deliverer!

10

Deliverance from a Dungeon

The Two Men
Matt. 9:27-31

For as long as we can remember, we have been in our own jail, our inner dungeon of blindness. But we don't know why. Smith's *Dictionary* says it could be "by quantities of dust and sand, pulverized by the intense heat of the sun; by the perpetual glare of the light; by the contrast between the heat and the cold sea air on the coast, by the dews at night while people sleep on the roofs, by smallpox."

Eyesight is one of our five senses. While our sense of hearing is sharper, to be blind is a severe handicap. We remember reading about the Philistines who gouged out Samson's eyes to make him harmless. As we shared the same handicap, so we shared the same sorrow. In fact, equal sorrow drove us together.

Matthew alone records our story of deliverance. It is believed to have happened in Peter's house in Capernaum.

Isaiah predicted the healing of the blind in the days of Christ (Isa. 29:18; 35:5).

After leaving Jairus' house, we followed Jesus, tapping our canes and shouting, "Have mercy on us, Son of David!" Being Jews, we wanted His attention and healing. After all, He is our coming Messiah (John 7:47), or Son of David, the anointed of God (2 Tim. 2:8).

Why did we call for mercy? Because mercy is in the character of God. It includes His compassion, pardon and forgiveness – the very qualities which sinners and the diseased need.

That's what we wanted. Needed. We craved God's controlling presence to show us mercy and love, redemption and faithfulness.

We first requested His mercy because we did not have any merit of our own. In fact, we were ranked with beggars. Begging was our trade. But, we had no right to grumble.

We are not sure where we first heard of Jesus. It could have been in our synagogue in Nazareth where He said He came to give sight to the blind.

We joined Jesus after He had entered the house. Then, no doubt to spur our faith, Jesus asked, "Do you believe that I am able to do this?" And we responded with, "Yes, Lord." That is, we expressed an eager faith in Him and in His power to open our eyes. R. C. Trench says that such faith is "the conducting link between man's emptiness and God's fullness ... the bucket let down into the fountain of God's grace without which the man could not draw up out of that fountain; the purse which does not itself make its owner rich, but which yet effectually enriches him by the treasure which it contains."

Whatever the source of our blindness, our focus was that He was able. His greatness was adequate to respond to our faith.

At once, Jesus touched our eyes, saying, "According to your faith will it be done to you." We would not be disappointed. Based on our faith in Christ's promises, He would heal us. According to Alexander Maclaren, faith, which works within His promises, "decides how much of Christ we shall have for our very own. Faith that goes outside Christ's promises is not faith."

In His healing miracles, Jesus used various methods. Here, He touched our eyes. Obviously, our faith was not in His look of compassion for we could not see His face. So, He must touch us for our faith and His healing to have a conduit for travel. Besides, He wanted to have a personal relationship and establish an intimate solidarity with us.

When Jesus opened our eyes, He gave us a stern warning, "See that no one knows about this." Why not? Because He does not want human praise to distract us from our Deliverer. Nor does He want His popularity to rush Him to the Cross. But how could we keep quiet? We were recipients of His sovereign power.

Then, says Matthew, we "went out and spread the news about him all over that region." Actually, we did not have to take the initiative to tell anyone. But, when asked who had opened our eyes, we simply confessed, "Jesus, the Miracle Worker." To say "The Son of David, the Messiah" would suggest He was in competition with Caesar, and that could start a religious riot.

No doubt, Jesus, for privacy, took us into the house. Calling Him the Son of David in public would be regarded as a political statement. Besides, Jesus dreaded popular excitement.

That's our story of deliverance.

11

Deliverance for the Dumb

The Speech-impaired Man
Luke 11:14-26

My story is quite complex. You see, before my deliverance I was blind and dumb. I could not talk, let alone tell my story. Without verbal and visual communication, my world was meaningless. The source of my muteness is unknown. Keith F. Nickle says it "could have been the result of an act of God ... (It could also be simply a natural disorder)."

However, the cause of my handicap was demon possession, which left me lonely and tormented. It took my human glory and tried to eradicate the image of God. I hardly knew what it was to be a human, especially a man.

According to David Gooding, "As originally made, man was intended to hold converse with God. Conscious of himself and of God, man could consciously respond to the Creator, and communicate in words with him who is the Word ... If it is God's desire and design, and man's chief glory, that he should be the priest of creation and articulate creation's response to the Creator, that he should talk with God as a son with a father, then it is obvious why it should be of prime strategic importance to the enemy to cripple man's ability to speak with God, to lock up man's spirit within himself, and as far as God is concerned to turn this earth into (to borrow a phrase) a silent planet."

I was not aware of any possibility of a cure. Besides, the demon would not let me think of such things. Seven hundred years before Jesus, Isaiah predicted that miracles would happen in the Messianic age. However, the Old Testament does not record any blind person receiving sight. But, some of my friends heard about Jesus, the Healer from Nazareth, and brought me to Him.

Jesus immediately took charge of my situation. Without any request from me, He expelled the demon and restored me to sanity. I experienced a transformation. A second ago I was blind and could not talk, but now I can see and speak. I was delivered and the crowd was amazed. Actually, "three responses follow: the crowd marvels, some critics question the source of Jesus' power, and others call for a sign as proof."

Beelzebul is Greek, but in Hebrew it is *Baalzebul*. It has two meanings: "lord of flies" and "lord of the dwelling." Baal, the prince, was the chief god of the Philistine city of Ekron. Beelzebul is also a title given to the highest god of the pagan *baals*. In Judaism, it was called Beelzebub, a title for Satan, the prince of devils. Eventually, "Since Jesus' enemies would not admit that he came from God, they attributed his power over demons to a superdemonic source." This was blasphemy, that is, saying that heaven's power came from hell.

Jesus' enemies wanted a sign from heaven, but they would not accept the sign or miracle Jesus had performed. If He was from heaven, then they wanted a heavenly sign, like a rearrangement of the sun, moon and stars, not just the casting out of a demon. They wanted a sign to convince them against their will.

Jesus knew what His enemies were thinking and replied: "Any kingdom divided against itself will be ruined, and a house divided against itself will fall." That is, if Satan gave Jesus power, Satan would be attacking himself. As Ray Summers explains, "So, if Satan ... divides his forces in order that they may fight against one another, he will be engaged in destroying his own kingdom."

Jesus could be referring to the Jewish nation when it was divided in the time of Jeroboam. In fact, Israel struggled with internal strife right up to the destruction of Jerusalem in A.D. 70. It's as if Jesus is saying, a church which professes unity, but is divided into fighting factions, loses its unity and falls. Furthermore, Jesus explained, "If Satan is divided against himself, how can his kingdom stand? I say this because you claim that I drive out demons by Beelzebub." If that is so, it's foolish, because Satan would be undoing his own work.

Jesus continued, "Now if I drive out demons by Beelzebub, by whom do your followers drive them out? So then, they will be your judges." That is, the followers of the Pharisees claimed to drive out demons by the power of God, and that was Jesus' claim, as well. An old proverb says, as Herbert Lockyer records, "The saint who works no miracles has few pilgrims." Therefore, to accuse Jesus of using satanic power was to condemn their followers, as well. And they, your judges, or witnesses against you, in turn will condemn you for accusing them.

Jesus told them, "But if I drive out demons by the finger of God, then the kingdom of God has come to you." Jesus was not saying *if* he drove demons out by the finger of God, but *since*, or that he was actually using God's power, not Satan's. So, for Jesus to use the power of God's Holy Spirit, even as little as His finger, was to bring the rule of God among them. It certainly was not by any kind of black magic. It was the same power as was demonstrated in the Exodus when Pharaoh's magicians recognized the power of God (Ex. 8:19; Deut. 9:10). In other words, because Jesus, their King, was present, the powers of evil were being overthrown.

Jesus proceeded to explain to them that, "When a strong man, fully armed, guards his own house, his possessions are safe." In other words,

Satan is the strongman who tries to protect his dominion and keep his possessions in his grasp.

"But," said Jesus, "when someone stronger attacks and overpowers him, he takes away the armour in which the man trusted and divides up the spoils." Jesus presented Himself as superior to Satan and able to release men from Satan's power. Therefore, He does not cast out demons by Satan's power, but by God's power.

To elaborate further, Jesus says, "He who is not with me is against me, and he who does not gather with me, scatters." That is, this is a positive or negative issue. If a person does not support Jesus, he opposes Him. We cannot be neutral. In Luke 9:50, a man was unconsciously cooperative with Jesus, but here some are consciously opposed. It all comes down to obedience. As Walter L. Liefeld explains: "Obedience to God's word is more important than even the closest human ties to Jesus." Jesus' hearers must choose.

Jesus then declares, "When an evil spirit comes out of a man, it goes through arid places seeking rest and does not find it. Then it says, 'I will return to the house I left.'" *Evil spirit* is a Jewish term for *demon*. Jesus is probably referring to the Jewish exorcists who claimed to cast out demons, but rejected the kingdom of God. The vacuum left when evil comes out of a man must be filled with that which is good, or else the evil will return. Oh the futility of spiritual emptiness!

Jesus says, "When it arrives, it finds the house swept clean and put in order." He is referring to a life cleaned, but unoccupied and lacking God's presence, which is open to an intrusion of evil.

Jesus concludes, "Then it goes and takes seven other spirits more wicked than itself, and they go in and live there. And the final condition of that man is worse than the first."

12

Deliverance for the Deranged

The Demoniac of Gadara
Mark 5:1-20

My name is Legion, and people always avoided me. They feared me and treated me as an assassin, not as a victim. I was bullied, trapped and driven. I did not deliberately choose to be possessed. In fact, I would have accepted deliverance.

One day, just after sunset, Jesus and His disciples set sail in several boats to cross the Sea of Galilee. En route, they encountered such a storm of wind that the boats were almost swamped. However, Jesus rebuked the savage wind and waves, saying, "Quiet! Be still!" (Mark 4:39). At once, the sea became calm.

After sailing for about five miles, they reached the other side and landed at Gadara, about six miles to the southeast. There, they encountered a wild man controlled by an inner storm. To paraphrase David L. McKenna, he worshipped while cursing and confessed while blaspheming. I was that man.

Gadara is inhabited by Gentiles of the Gerasenes and their pig farms. Also, within a two-mile radius are a number of tombs carved in the hillside and a steep slope forty yards from shore. Those tombs, or graves of the dead, were for the poor and the many demented people who lived among them. It was a spooky place.

That's where I lived, if you can call it living. At least, that's where I existed, but not by my own choice. You see, I was controlled by a demon, or an unclean spirit, which is morally filthy, affecting my mind and my vocabulary. According to G. Campbell Morgan, "The Greeks believed they were the spirits of departed men ..."

I was extremely strong and could not be bound, not even with a chain. I was beyond restraint. R. Kent Hughes describes me like this: "The local townspeople had attempted to restrain him, but with terrifying herculean strength he had broken the fetters which bound him. He was uncontrollable and dangerous. Inside, he was totally wretched. At intervals during the night and day he would let out a preternatural howl, then gash himself with jagged rocks in an obvious attempt to drive out the evil spirits."

Over time, different people had tried to bind me with metal shackles around my ankles and iron chains around my upper body. However, I broke them all to pieces. David A. Redding says, "Legion is Samson gone berserk."

With my weird and fierce mannerisms, I became a terror to those living in the area. Night and day, I routinely screamed and slashed myself with sharp stones. I certainly had all the "four characteristics of a madman: walking abroad at night, spending the night on a grave, tearing one's clothes and destroying what one was given" (Talmud). I was in a hopeless situation – trapped in torment and headed for destruction as the image of God.

Strange as it may seem, I knew what I was doing, but I was like a puppet, controlled by someone else. I often ran wild, naked and screaming.

As Ivan Turgenev explains, "I do not know what the heart of a bad man is like, but I know what the heart of a good man is like...and it is terrible."

The disciples were between a rock and a hard place. Simon J. Kistemaker says, "The disciples had just faced the tempest on the lake, and now they faced the tempest of a fierce man with enormous physical strength. Jesus had shown them violence in nature on the lake; now He made them encounter demonic power on land." Seeing Jesus from a distance, I was propelled toward Him and fell on my knees to pay Him reverence. But, this was the demon's way to get Jesus' attention and confront Him.

The demon brazenly asked Jesus, "What do you want with me, Jesus, Son of the Most High God? Swear to God that you won't torture me!" By this title, the demon was acknowledging Christ's divine origin. He was also thinking that, by using Christ's name, he had control over Him (Mark 1:24). Actually, the demon inside me was asking, "What do we have in common?" The fact is, Jesus believed in the Devil as the head of the spiritual underworld. Jesus knew his evil tactics. And, He knew the demon was speaking through me and commanded, "Come out of this man, you evil spirit!" As David A. Redding comments, "Jesus acted as if emergencies were made for His miracles." Realizing Jesus' power, the demon knew it was time to leave.

At that point, Jesus asked, "What is your name?" That is, "What are you usually called?" The demon answered, "My name is Legion, for we are many." Then he pled with Jesus that He would not send them out of the area.

The demon had a plural name, referring to a Roman legion of six thousand men. He was admitting to being possessed by numerous demons, all in opposition to Jesus, and all as one combined force.

Why did Jesus want to know my name? Redding answers, "Jesus was seeking power over him by trying to understand the power that was controlling him ... An Indian bride frequently will not give up her name to her bridegroom until after their marriage, when alone he has any rights or power over her. We remember that in the old Genesis story, the angel asks Jacob his name, and Jacob gives it. But when Jacob says to the angel, 'Tell me thy name,' no name is given. The angel had power over Jacob.

Jacob had no power over the angel. Savages will rarely disclose their true names, for similar reasons."

William Barclay writes, "There was a Jewish saying, 'A legion of hurtful spirits is on the watch for men, saying, "When shall he fall into the hands of one of these things and be taken?"'"

I grew up in a time when the military legions were rough and ready, and guilty of horror and violence that would make the blood run cold. I had seen suffering and murder on such a wide scale that it opened the door for my demon possession. Therefore, I would need a foolproof demonstration to convince me that my demon had left. And, I got that proof when all two thousand pigs scampered down the hill and drowned in the sea.

According to Herbert Lockyer, "the Devil's power is exercised ... directly, by himself, by the demons who are subject to their prince, and through human beings whom he has influenced and possesses." I became Satan's victim when one of his demons invaded my personality. Somewhere, I had let down my guard, giving the demon opportunity to enter and control me.

I learned quite early that all demons are afraid that Jesus will send them into eternal punishment before their time (Luke 8:31). As a second option, Legion asked Jesus not to send us out of the area, but to let us enter a herd of pigs, unclean to Jews. Jesus gave us permission, and our whole herd stampeded down a steep slope and drowned in the lake (Matt. 8:32).

Redding explains: "That the swine were driven into the sea was no work of the divine miracle, but was the work of the demons by divine permission." This was a real object lesson, showing the extent of evil from which I had been delivered.

As you can surmise, this caused quite a stir in the entire countryside. The Gentile pig farmers scattered in all directions, spreading the story of the demonized hogs. Consequently, people came from near and far to see for themselves. Years later, that area became desert, inhabited by the Troglodytes, a wild savage people living in tombs.

They expected to see Jesus and me, Legion, and were surprised to see me sitting, contented and comfortable, dressed and in my right mind. It scared them. Instead of roaming and running, I was relaxed, ready to be Jesus' disciple. Instead of being naked, I was dressed and decent enough to re-enter society. Instead of being wild and screaming, I was ready to take responsibility for my family.

In my day, to clothe a man was to adopt him. So, since Jesus cured and clothed me, I assumed I was to stay with Him. Like the prodigal son to whom his father gave the best robe, I was still part of my family. This is why Jesus suggested that I go home. My adoption was legitimate.

Previously, the demons were afraid of Jesus. Now, the people are afraid of Jesus and the remarkable power that had cured me. Those who witnessed the dramatic event spread the remarkable story of what had happened to me and the pigs. Surprisingly, the people urged Jesus to leave the area. They were fearful of possible negative repercussions on their property and finances. Besides, they did not want Christ's power to disrupt their ungodly living.

When Jesus was getting into a boat to leave the area, I requested to go with Him. But He refused my request, saying, "Go home to your family and tell them how much the Lord has done for you, and how he has had mercy on you." That was all I needed. So, I started in Decapolis, Greek cities east of the Jordan River, telling my amazing story of deliverance. After all, as Donald W. Burdick writes, "Man is not delivered from bondage merely for his own enjoyment of God-given freedom, but also that he may give testimony to others concerning the divine Deliverer."

Jesus refused my request to go with Him because He had not delivered me for show, nor as a projection of Himself. As Herbert Lockyer says, Jesus "wanted this man to function as a memorial of His grace among his own friends and family, and to bring them to repentance." After all, while Jesus can command evil spirits, He can only plead with human hearts.

Those cities were in Syria, and if Jesus was there, it was a sign of good things to come. For, with Him there, Jews would be there. Consequently, Christianity would break the bonds of Judaism. Now you know why Jesus sent me back to my family to share my wonderful story of deliverance!

13

Deliverance from Death

Jarius' Daughter
Mark 5:21-24; 35-42

I am Jarius, a leading ruler in the local synagogue at Capernaum. I was responsible for arranging the services, lecturing and giving direction to the elders. I was not a priest, but a layman.

Jesus and His disciples returned to the northwest side of the Sea of Galilee, to Capernaum (Matt. 9:1), which had been His headquarters since being rejected at Nazareth (Luke 4:31).

I was not a follower of Jesus, but I knew the truth when I heard it. And, I knew a miracle when I saw one. Besides, I had a need – my daughter was dying. That's why I went to Jesus.

A child's death is always traumatic, but that of an *only* child is tragic. In my distress, I felt the powerlessness of my legal religion. But, in Jesus, I sensed concern and hope. As Alexander Maclaren points out, I was "driven by despair, but drawn by trust."

G. Campbell Morgan cites Charles Kingsley, who "declared that the death of a soldier is touched with heroism, the death of an old man is surrounded with glory of completion; but the death of a child demonstrates something wrong somewhere."

I admit I was prejudiced about Jesus. That is, I judged Him before I examined the evidence, and cut myself and my family off from many blessings.

However, I had to abandon my prejudice and swallow my pride. So, in desperation, and without apology, I threw myself at Jesus' feet. Regardless of losing my position in the synagogue and my prestige in Capernaum, I had to get help for my dying twelve-year-old daughter. As they say, "Blood is thicker than water."

Jesus responded immediately. Before I finished asking Him to come to my house, He was out the door. Not a moment must be lost. He was now in control.

But, it was not to be, at least, not yet. We faced an obstacle, an interruption – a woman with a serious hemorrhage stopped Jesus in His tracks! She had suffered for twelve years and was getting worse. When she heard about Jesus, she pushed her way through the crowd and touched His cloak, thinking, "If I just touch his clothes, I will be healed." Her healing was immediate.

At that moment, my friends approached, saying, "Your daughter is dead. Why bother the teacher anymore?" Jesus, ignoring what the friends had reported, encouraged me with "Don't be afraid; just believe." That is, continue to believe. Myron S. Augsburger contends that "faith for healing is faith in Christ, not faith as a psychological influence that serves to induce healing."

When I was told my daughter had died, I did not want to believe it. Some expected me to give up, but how could I? This was the crucial point for the miracle. As David A. Redding says, "Death always makes a weak ending to a tragedy."

Peter, James and John made up Jesus' inner circle of faith and fellowship. He allowed them, along with my wife and me, to go to our daughter's side.

To this point, I was helpless. That's a low blow for any man, especially a father. And, particularly a ruler of the synagogue, who is supposed to have all the answers.

Weeping and wailing were proof that death had taken our daughter. The female mourners and musicians were hired and paid for their services for that day only. So their crying was loud and public. Our little girl had to be buried that day.

Although Jesus used the word *asleep*, He was saying that while her body was dead, her resurrection would be as simple as waking her.

As for my daughter being *asleep*, Jerome says, "'She is not dead but sleeps' because to God all things live." As Bede concludes: "To men who could not quicken, she is dead; to God she is asleep." In fact, when He had come, death was, from that time forward, a sleep. Simon J. Kistemaker comments: "A father believed that Jesus was stronger than death ... The death-defying faith of this father teaches that Jesus' reach is as deep as death."

Mourning by weeping and moaning may be cultural, but it is not proper when one is about to wake from sleep. True grief is silent. Like Lazarus (John 11:11), my daughter's body needed a resurrection from physical death. Besides, as Herbert Lockyer explains: "*sleep* is only used of the body of the dead – never of the soul."

While most of their mourning was artificial, their laughing was in Jesus' face, a laugh of scorn to humiliate Him. They were sure the girl's death could not be reversed.

Jesus forbids all weeping and expressions of sorrow only after He has removed its cause. After all, tears have a way of purging our hearts.

When Jesus put the mourners out, it was as if He had shown them the door. It reminds me of the sign two college students had on the inside of their dorm door, "You can brighten up this room by leaving it." Just so, those unbelieving mourners did not deserve to see a miracle. Such a death-room, according to Lockyer, is "no place for boisterous and superfluous grief."

Jesus allowed only my wife and me, along with Peter, James and John, to stay with the child. He then took her hand and, speaking Aramaic, said, "'Talitha koum!' (which means, 'Little girl, I say to you, get up!')." She did, and her life and personality returned immediately.

When Jesus told my daughter to get up, her spirit returned. Some people believed quite strongly that "a person's spirit lingered about for three days after death hoping to get back into the body, but on the fourth day when the natural processes of death had definitely taken over the body, the spirit would go away. That was Martha's meaning when, concerning Lazarus, she said, 'Lord ... he has been dead four days' (John 11:39). Her concern was not so much with the unpleasant situation of opening the cave after those processes had started as it was with the fact that *it was too late* for Lazarus. She, too, learned that when Jesus is present, it is never too late."

Michael Lloyd points out that God "likes to be with hurt people, despised people, ignored people, sinful people, crushed people, real people."

Jesus had the last word over life and death. He did not revive her, He resurrected her. He, the Lord of life, spoke a brief word and, as Lockyer writes: "The spirit of the damsel returned from the unseen world and became reunited with her body." Her spirit had never died. When the people saw her walking, they were astounded.

Jesus warned us to keep this miracle secret. He did not want to display His miraculous power to make Him a popular political figure. Lockyer points out that Jesus' miracles were not meant "to satisfy curiosity or merely to compel belief or overawe mankind." But Jesus told us to give her something to eat.

Miracles are like that. They may be slow coming, but they are real and they are done. For me, my doubt and questions are in the past. I am relieved and my daughter is alive!

14

Deliverance from Disease

The Hemorrhaging Daughter
Mark 5:25-34

My story begins with Jesus en route to Jarius' house to raise his twelve-year-old daughter from death. I interrupted His journey for my own personal deliverance. For twelve years I had wished I was dead. In fact, I had visited doctors near and far, and exhausted my life savings in search of a cure. But, without a miracle, I was desperate and driven to despair.

I was embarrassed and ashamed. My dignity and self-worth were gone. And my pale complexion was a telltale sign that showed everyone I was sick.

Richard Exley explains: "How this could have happened to me I do not know. I was always healthy. That is until I gave birth to my first child.

Though the birth was not difficult as births go, I was never able to recover. As the weeks passed with no sign of improvement, I experienced a growing concern, but even then I was not alarmed. Whatever concern I may have had was soon forgotten in the joy of motherhood. Of course I was tired all of the time but, I reasoned, what mother of a newborn isn't?

"Although my physical condition wore on me, the hardest part was being segregated, ostracized really. According to the Law of Moses, I was ceremonially unclean and anyone or anything I touched became unclean. Of course I could not be intimate with my husband nor could I worship in the Temple or in the synagogue."

I had visited physicians from Caesarea Philippi to Capernaum, trying all kinds of cures, including home remedies, but nothing worked. Doctors were baffled and I gradually grew worse.

Hemorrhaging, especially for a woman, is not something to make public. It's always an unspoken prayer request. So, without anyone knowing, I had to secretly get to Jesus and touch Him.

In Jesus' day, devout Jews wore an outer robe with four tassels, attached to a blue ribbon at the bottom or hem (Num. 15:37-40). Those tassels identified a man as chosen by God (Deut. 22:12). My goal was to touch one of those tassels.

When I heard about Jesus, I watched for an opportunity to touch Him, if only to touch His clothes. My thinking was, "If I just touch his clothes, I will be healed." As a woman, I had no standing or position; and being unclean, I was an outcast – divorced and discarded.

My bleeding classified me as unclean. Whatever I touched and wherever I sat were unclean (Lev. 15:25-27). My family shunned me and society abandoned me, barring me from the synagogue and Temple. I was an outcast and lived alone.

While my hemorrhaging was abnormal, I did not know the internal cause. Nor did I know much about Jesus, especially as to how He healed. But, I knew my body and its continuous dysfunction. Plus, I knew the inability of the doctors to cure my affliction. So, I had to direct my faith to the One with compassion and power to heal, and who also had a good track record of multiple cures.

At that point, I did not know what to expect, but Jesus' response was all I needed. Actually, His question put me on the spot. When I reached out to touch Jesus' cloak, I felt a surge of power all through my body. And, He felt it too as it left His body. In fact, He asked, "Who touched my clothes?" Undoubtedly, He knew it was me, but He wanted me to identify myself and give God thanks. He challenged me to make my healing known, not through superstition and magic, but through one touch of faith.

Of course, feeling healing power leave Jesus' body did not mean He had lost power. After all, being divine means He cannot lose power. Rather, God's power was transferred through Him. Consequently, He was sensitive to my "anxious tug of faith" in spite of the "casual bumps of the jostling crowd." He willingly gave something of himself to meet my desperate human need.

Jesus' question, "Who touched my clothes?," got my attention. Was He suggesting that touching made Him unclean? Was He saying that healing does not come just by touching some material object? Or, was He implying that healing does not come without a personal relationship with Jesus? Some believe I thought my faith was magic. But no, my faith was in Jesus, not in His fabric. Mine was a faith venture in a time of great need.

The truth is, I knew that if I could touch Him, He would help me. It was a risk on my part, but I figured He might overlook my uncleanness, and even touch me in return. After all, many people were rubbing shoulders with Jesus and touching Him accidentally, but I touched Him on purpose.

It must have been obvious that I was desperate for healing. Most in the crowd were interested in Jesus socially, politically and religiously. But I was interested in Him personally. I expected a miracle! So, as Augustine suggested, while flesh was *pressing* Jesus, my faith was *touching* Him.

The disciples, thinking Jesus' question was silly, retorted, "You see the people crowding against you, and yet you can ask, 'Who touched me?'" To Jesus, a crowd was never a mob.

When I realized I should not keep silent, I had no other choice but to admit I was the one who had touched Him. So, I fell at His feet and, trembling with fear, told Him the whole truth regarding my miracle. To me, necessity knows no law. Besides, as G. Campbell Morgan put it, "contact that heals must always issue in confession that glorifies." Such deliberate contact always receives a deliberate answer. My bleeding stopped immediately and I felt clean.

The songwriter, George F. Root, encourages all of us to *touch* Christ and expect deliverance.

That's when Jesus said to me, "Daughter, your faith has healed you. Go in peace and be freed from your suffering." Actually, He recognized my faith by the courage I took to follow Him and touch His clothes. So, by calling me *daughter*, He adopted me into God's family and challenged me to continue living the life of expectancy.

I am so thankful that Jesus did not mention my disease. What He delivered me from does not matter. He is the healer of both private and public needs, everything from headaches to hemorrhaging. I discovered, in the words of Frederick Dale Bruner, that "Jesus is present wherever there is faith in Him." My faith was not in touching His robe, but in trusting Him. After all, godly faith gets its substance from the person it trusts.

I feel as though I represent humanity, for we are all sick in some way. And, we spend our time and money trying one cure after another. Well, take it from me, Jesus is the answer. His death and resurrection provide the pardon, healing and hope we desperately need. All that is required is our touch of faith. And, believe me, Jesus answers all faith according to His will and regardless of our weak appeal.

There are needy people willing to exercise faith for a miracle. F. B. Meyer says that "Faith receives as much as it desires."

I learned three lessons from my deliverance. As Myron S. Augsburger states, Jesus' "goodness turns our problems into occasions of hope ... His greatness makes our needs seem small ... His graciousness makes our healing sure."

15

Deliverance for a Daughter

The Canaanite Girl
Mark 7:24-30

When Jesus left Capernaum, He walked thirty-five miles northwest to the area of Tyre and Sidon, two Gentile seaport cities in Phoenicia, on the Mediterranean seacoast. They were a part of Syria, but are now modern Lebanon. *Tyre* means *the Rock* because, as William Barclay says, "off the shore lay two great rocks joined by a three-thousand-feet-long ridge," forming a natural breakwater and harbour.

I'm a Syrophoenican woman, a descendant of the Canaanites, the accursed race once doomed of God. I worshipped the great mother-goddess, Ashtoreth, or queen of heaven, who was supposed to give her devotees everything good and permit them to do almost everything evil. Because I am Greek, I am a pagan and not part of the Jewish covenant. I belong to a despised population with whom Israel was to have no dealings (Ezra 9:1-12). In fact, I was, in David A. Redding's words, "the lowest breed of Gentile, one of Baal's illicit daughters."

It is somewhat mysterious that Jesus' only trip beyond Israel's borders would be to Tyre and Sidon, especially since He had said those cities were hard places (Matt. 11:21). In fact, according to G. Campbell Morgan, they were once considered to be under God's curse. But, since Jesus came to minister to the heathen, I was one of them.

However, there was, in that very area, a woman who needed an act of mercy ... me. As G. Campbell Morgan writes, "one of the sweetest stories of them all – the mother's heart carrying the need of her daughter with unswerving faith to Him who had created the love of the mother."

My story of deliverance is actually my daughter's story. She was delivered from a demon. That is, a fallen spirit had taken control of her, leaving her body twisted and contorted, rendering her "possessed by an evil spirit."

My daughter's miracle began with my faith in Jesus. Mark recalls that He commended me for my great faith. Obviously, my faith pleased Him. The truth is, my faith is my own, completely opposite to the unbelief of the scribes and Pharisees. It is bold, for I did not hesitate to have a conversation with a man, especially Jesus. "In fact," R. Kent Hughes writes, "there was at this time a strict sect called 'The Bruised and Bleeding Pharisees' because every time they saw a woman they covered their eyes, and thus bumped into whatever happened to be about."

The odds were against me from the start. I was a Gentile, not a Jew. As a woman, I was not allowed to speak to a man. And, I lived in a pagan culture and worshipped heathen gods. Besides, I did not have previous contact with Jesus, hearing only that He could cast out demons.

When I heard of Christ, I went to Him and, falling at His feet, pled for my daughter. After all, hearing was not enough. Hearing of water does not quench thirst. Nor does hearing of medicine heal disease.

In Tyre, Jesus stayed in a house in which He hoped to escape notice for a while. But word spread that He was in the area. Besides, He was in

Gentile territory, wanting to meet with His disciples for rest, peace and quiet. At least He would be out of Herod's jurisdiction.

Why was it significant for Jesus to be in Gentile territory? Well, just as He eliminated the distinction between clean and unclean foods, so He eliminated the difference between clean and unclean people. In other words, the gospel is for the whosoever.

Actually, under Joshua, this Gentile territory had been allocated to Israel as far as Tyre and Sidon (Josh. 19:28-29). However, Israel had been unable to claim it. Jesus, the true Israel, came among the Gentiles to claim His inheritance.

The question remains, why did Jesus travel outside Israel to Tyre and Sidon? No doubt, after extending privileges to Israel, the time had come for Him to offer blessings to the Gentiles, the "other sheep" (John 10:16), "the lost sheep of Israel" (Matt. 10:6). He would not hinder the lost sheep of the Gentile world from coming to Him, nor would He send them away.

As for Jesus hiding himself, Herbert Lockyer observes, "The more He tried to conceal himself, the more He became known. Who can hide the glory of the sun? As Light, Jesus could not be buried in a world of darkness. So great a physician could not go unnoticed in a world of suffering." Besides, how could He remain hidden when a mother was outside, in agony over her daughter?

For some reason, Jesus wanted to reduce His public ministry for a while. In spite of that, hundreds of people came to hear Him preach and bring their sick to be healed. However, Jesus did not want to be seen merely as a miracle worker or a divine man. Neither did He want God's power reduced to magic and superstition.

When I heard where Jesus was staying, I rushed there in aggressive pursuit on behalf of my daughter. Distress has a way of quickening our hearing. I fell at Jesus' feet, begging him to drive the demon out of her. After all, I knew that Jesus could do what medical doctors could not do. So, I persevered for her deliverance. Actually, I made her misery my own, pleading, "Lord, Son of David, have mercy on me! My daughter is suffering terribly from demon-possession" (Matt. 15:22).

To my amazement, Jesus responded with silence and what appeared to be indifference. I felt He acted cold towards me. Was He trying to remain hidden, evading me and my need? Did He need more time to consider my request? Martin Luther writes, "Now he is as silent as a stone." At least He didn't say, "No." Nor was He leaving it to chance. For there is no luck, chance or accident in God's Kingdom.

However, I was not silent. Neither were the impatient disciples. In fact, they urged Him, "Send her away, for she keeps crying out after us" (Matt. 15:23). Peter probably scowled, John was impatient, and Andrew and Philip thought I was rude.

Although I was surprised, I took no offense at Jesus' answer. Actually, I was pleased. He replied, "It is not right to take the children's bread and toss it to their dogs" (Matt. 15:26). To quote Alyce M. McKenzie, it is always God's will "that society's vulnerable, the women and children, be fed both physically and spiritually."

This was a test of my faith, patience and perseverance. After all, Jesus' preaching must first be to the children of Israel (Rom. 1:16), the Jewish people in God's covenant. The children's bread is God's blessing on the Jews (Matt. 8:12).

What does Jesus mean by referring to *dogs*? He likened me to a household pet. That meant I had a master. I was not a wild, ferocious dog of the street, a scavenger, but a loving and obedient pet. In fact, as William L. Lane writes, "if the dogs eat the crumbs under the table, they are fed *at the same time* as the children." I would be satisfied with a single crumb of power and grace from His table.

The dog was a symbol of dishonour, which is why a woman of the street was called a dog. Sometimes, *dog* was a Jewish term to demean and insult Gentiles. Similarly, the nations of the world are compared to dogs, as Isaiah writes, "dogs with mighty appetites" (Isa. 56:11).

In his response to me, Jesus did not use the word for a wild dog of the street, but a little house dog. He spoke affectionately to me, explaining that the children must be fed first, followed by the pets. That is, Israel first, then the Gentiles could eat what the Jews rejected. Besides, Jesus had to be careful not to give the impression that He was abandoning Israel (cf. Matt. 4:24; 8:5).

I quickly said, "Yes, Lord, but even the dogs eat the crumbs that fall from their masters' table" (Matt. 15:27). When I expressed such faith, Jesus detected my humility.

Out of respect for Jesus' deity, I called Him Lord. I recognized Him as the universal prophet from Nazareth. He alone could show mercy to me and deliverance for my daughter.

Then Jesus made this positive declaration, "For such a reply, you may go; the demon has left your daughter." Obviously, my faith was more important than what Simon J. Kistemaker calls "racial and national boundaries." No doubt this promise of deliverance has been extended to the Church around the world.

When I returned home, my daughter was on the bed and delivered from the demon. A. J. Maxham, in *Thy Daughter is Free*, describes her deliverance:

She came unto Jesus, her heart filled with grief,
She called to Him, "Master, O grant my relief;
My daughter is sick, she is sorely oppressed;
O grant my petition and heal her distress."

Her cry was unheeded, in vain did she pray,
Until His disciples said, "Send her away";
Then Jesus rebukingly said, "Not to thee,
To the lost sheep of Israel, salvation is free."

"'Tis time, Lord and Master, yet, O hear my prayer,
I ask but for crumbs from Thy table to share;
Thou surely wilt not send me empty away;
O hear my petition, and heal her today."

Then Jesus spake to her, in tones all divine,
"Be it as thou wilt and no longer repine;
So great is thy faith, be it now unto thee,
All things that thou asketh, thy daughter is free."

16

Deliverance for the Deaf

The Man of Decapolis
Mark 7:31-37

From Tyre and Sidon, Jesus travelled twenty-five miles north, deep into Gentile territory. He then headed south to the east side of the Sea of Galilee into the middle of Decapolis. Herod Antipas was still ruling and people wanted to force Jesus to be king.

Decapolis "consisted of ten Gentile cities which had been granted special privileges by the Roman conquerors about a century earlier." Jesus went up on a mountainside to rest. However, large "crowds came to him, bringing the lame, the blind, the crippled, the mute and many others, and laid them at his feet, and he healed them" (Matt. 15:30). This started a chain reaction of healings and praise to God.

I lived in Decapolis and had a severe handicap – I was deaf and could not talk. Most people called me deaf and dumb. Some of my friends brought me to Jesus for Him to lay His hands on me and heal me.

R. Kent Hughes explains: "Terrible as blindness is, the blind do not suffer the social pain and stigma experienced by the deaf – the gawking, impatient stares of those who are not aware of one's condition. There is also the humiliation of being thought stupid because one cannot understand or speak."

I was a deaf-mute for as long as I can remember. Herbert Lockyer describes my condition, writing, "at least he was incapable of uttering articulate sounds ... Evidently the man had not been born deaf. If he had, he would not have been able to speak at all." No doubt his deafness became obvious later in life.

Compared to blindness, deafness is more severe. Deafness put me in a silent world, where communication was nil. Lockyer explains: "deafness to heaven soon betrays itself through a serious impediment in our speech. There is a dullness, a drab monotony in the tone of the voice of a man who misses the melody of the Kingdom. The life goes out of a man's vocabulary, religious words lose their luster, and the vibrance goes out of the hymns of him who has ceased to hear the Word of God."

According to Bishop Horsley, "Of all natural imperfections, deafness seems the most deplorable, as it is that which excludes the unhappy sufferer from society." And Hughes agrees, saying I was "in bondage to a terrible physical handicap."

Before laying His hands on me, Jesus took me away from the crowd so we could be alone. He then placed His fingers into my ears, a sign that He was preparing me for my healing. In other words, He understood me and my problem. I could not hear His explanation, but I felt His deliberate touch.

Why did Jesus take me away from the crowd? Specifically, to give me His complete attention. He did not want me to be influenced by the noise and emotion of numbers. He wanted me to receive my miracle for myself – alone with Jesus, privately. Consequently, He acted with common courtesy, and would not embarrass me for public show.

I learned an important lesson from this experience. That is, according to Herbert Lockyer, it "is good for us to be alone in the divine presence, away from the busy hum and din of a noisy world which is never conducive to spiritual reflection." In fact, I have found that it is important to establish contact in order to develop a personal relationship. Besides, creating privacy made me more receptive to the miraculous.

Then Jesus did something strange – He spat. And, when He touched my tongue, I knew He was about to restore my speech. I could not hear Him, but I could see and feel what He was doing. In fact, I could not speak properly because I could not hear.

But why did Jesus spit? If He spat on the ground, it was to show that the demon had left. For Him to spit on my tongue seemed out of character. But, most likely, Jesus spat on his own finger and then touched my tongue. This practice was common in many parts of the world.

Now it was time for Jesus to pray. So, He looked up to heaven to show me He was praying for me, and that He had a connection with the Divine. I could tell He was so close to God that His power was at my disposal. He was one with the Father and could claim divine help in His work of mercy. After all, as R. Kent Hughes writes, "Jesus was in constant communion with the Father, whether he was speaking to him or not."

In His prayer, Jesus groaned because the sight of human suffering touched His heart. He had feelings which could relate to hurting human beings. Only by looking to heaven could He bear the sight of earth. I could feel His empathy. I knew He was concerned. He expressed deep emotion. Our plight always moves Him to sigh with compassion.

At the conclusion of Jesus' prayer, He turned to me and, with a sigh, said, "'Ephphatha!' (which means, 'Be opened!')." His sigh was not a sign of weakness, but of strength and authority to act. His word was the utterance of His will. His sigh was such a gasp that, in the words of E. V. Riev, "He gave way to such distress of spirit as made His body tremble."

F. B. Meyer explains: "A sigh is one of the most touching and significant tokens of excessive grief. When our natures are too disturbed to remember to take a normal breath and must compensate for this omission by one deep-drawn breath, we sigh deeply in our spirit."

As I stood before Jesus, no doubt He could imagine all the spiritually deaf and dumb around Him. He knew all the sin and sorrow of mankind, and His sensitive heart responded with a heavy sigh.

Mark says my ears were opened, my tongue loosed and I began to speak plainly. Opening my ears and loosening the string of my tongue was part of what God would do to redeem His people. "Then will the eyes of the blind be opened and the ears of the deaf unstopped. Then will the lame leap like a deer, and the mute tongue shout for joy. Water will gush forth in the wilderness and streams in the desert" (Isa. 35:5-6).

This hands-on approach proved necessary for my healing. Likewise, as Hughes contends, "the hands-on touch is absolutely necessary to healthy, authentic Christianity."

For personal, and probably prophetic reasons, Jesus did not want to have a public ministry among the Gentiles. So, He commanded everyone to keep the miracle secret. Besides, this was the very area "where the people had tried to make Him king and so He cautioned the people to be quiet and avoid publicity."

As you can imagine, the crowd could not be silenced. In their astonishment, they exclaimed, "He has done everything well." From a woman's perspective, that is what the world needs to see today – competent Christians not merely doing good, but doing it well.

For my miracle, Jesus did all things so well that I would never doubt His healing ministry. He did not abhor "the contact of morality and disease and loathsome corruption; but laid His hands upon death, and it lived; upon sickness, and it was whole; on rotting leprosy, and it was sweet as the flesh of a little child."

17

Deliverance from Darkness

The Blind Man at Bethsaida
Mark 8:22-26

The city of Capernaum lies two miles north of Bethsaida, known as "the village," on the southeast shore of the Sea of Galilee (Mark 6:45). In Jesus' day, it was a large and prosperous town, as William L. Lane says, "the size of a city but the organization of a village."

Bethsaida, which was home to the fishermen, Peter, Andrew and Philip, was where Jesus performed many miracles. But, when He did not see any spiritual growth, He said Sodom and Gomorrah would not be judged as much as Bethsaida. After all, the people of Bethsaida, as those of Nazareth (Matt. 3:57-58), had resisted former miracles, therefore, they did not deserve another.

This is the record of a historical event. Mark alone relates my story, the story of a blind man living the life of a beggar. I was that blind man.

However, I had good friends, townspeople, who led me to Jesus. He would touch me and cure my blindness, one of the world's greatest curses. As Henry Gariepy explains, "One of the most serious afflictions in tropical countries is blindness. It is caused by accidents at birth in which skilled attention is lacking, or by glaring sunshine, dust, and infection, which local conditions favor."

According to E. R. Micklem, "Apparently those who brought him thought it was only necessary for Jesus to touch him in order to regain his sight. But Jesus was not a miraculous therapeutic machine: He dealt with individuals individually and personally and not in a mechanical way." Jesus never tried to display His miraculous power. But, He worked His miracles as the outcome of His contact with human need.

Showing His readiness to help me, and to avoid public excitement, Jesus grasped my hand and led me outside the village. He was very considerate. I felt He entered my mind and heart. Actually, His leading me was similar to God the Father leading Israel into the wilderness, so that He might speak to her heart.

Jesus established a personal relationship with me, giving me confidence to expect a miracle. For me, holding my hand was crucial. It was personal contact, the bridge to my deliverance.

In our privacy, Jesus put some of His saliva on my eyes and asked, "Do you see anything?" I replied, "I see people; they look like trees walking around."

I immediately but silently wondered why Jesus used spittle. J. N. Darby explains: "He uses that which was of Himself, that which possessed the efficacy of His own person to perform the cure." Besides, the spittle would separate my eyelids which were stuck together. This did not require a miracle, but restoring my sight did.

Herbert Lockyer says Jesus "was not bound to any one particular method of healing ... He was only clothing the supernatural in the form of the natural. As the omnipotent One, He could heal with or without means, because He Himself was the true Source of healing and life." At various times, Jesus' touch may vary, but God's grace remains the same.

Jesus used methods I could understand. I was the recipient of His free grace, in all its varied forms, especially in its gradual and progressive nature. Besides, as Joseph Parker notes, "All good men do not see God with equal quickness or equal clearness."

David A. McKenna points out: "Spiritual maturity is never instantaneous." But, spiritual enlightenment must always be progressive.

As you may suspect, I was set in my ways. I was not used to seeing things differently. My culture had me bound. As you would say, I had God in a box. Consequently, to me, Jesus' action was too odd and out of the ordinary. Why didn't He act in a more standard and uniform fashion? I imagine it was because if He had one standard mode of healing, I, and many others, would create a cult of formalism and make all miracles a ritual, not a relationship. We would not distinguish man from a tree.

The truth is, to receive God's highest gifts and to see His divine beauty, we must be alone with Him. Otherwise, we will not enter what two of your songwriters, S. F. Bennett and J. P. Webster, refer to as the "land that is fairer than day," nor see the King in all His beauty.

When Jesus saw I now had faith to be healed, He put His hands on my eyes a second time. At that point, my eyes immediately were opened and my sight was restored. I saw everything clearly, including people, even at a distance. I had 20/20 vision.

Incidentally, preparation for my miracle happened gradually. And, the first person I saw was Jesus. That's true spiritual growth. After all, Christian progress is not only seeing new things, but seeing the old and the new more clearly.

No doubt my healing was part of what God was doing in bringing salvation to Israel. Speaking of Israel's redemption, Isaiah writes, "Then will the eyes of the blind be opened and the ears of the deaf unstopped" (Isa. 35:5).

After my healing, Jesus said I should go home, not back to the village. He did not want to create a crisis before finishing His ministry. So, I was to avoid the crowd at all costs. Obviously, as David A. Redding writes, such "miracles were not His major work, but by-products of His loving power."

Having one's physical sight restored is similar to receiving one's spiritual eyesight. Someone has said: "When we are regenerated and the light breaks into us, it is as if we see things that we never saw before. Our whole outlook on life changes because of the touch of the Lord. But it is as if we see men as trees walking. We see, but we see imperfectly. From there we need another touch of Christ, and another, and another, so that our vision of the loveliness of Christ and of the presence of the kingdom of God becomes sharper and sharper."

In her poem, *The Second Touch,* Velma D. Collins writes that most of us grope our way through life and often need a second touch.

18

Deliverance from Degradation

The Demonic Boy
Mark 9:14-29

This is the story of glory on Mount Hermon, ending in gloom in the valley. The day after Jesus' transfiguration, He had to face His disciples' failure in the valley. Ecstasies had turned into demonical degradation. A father's only son was controlled by an evil spirit and acted like a maniac.

Whatever the situation, the God of the mountain is the God of the valley. But, we can't stay on the mountain. True, we need our solitude to keep contact with God, and we have to connect with our fellow man and cope with the demands of the valley. In fact, in the valley we practice and prove our Christianity.

Leaving the foretaste of millennial glory and the solemn voice of God the Father, Peter, James and John joined the other disciples in the valley. Among the large crowd, the unbelieving scribes, the teachers of the Law, were rudely arguing with the other nine disciples. Those scribes, no doubt sent by the Sanhedrin as witnesses, were hoping to find something against the disciples and prove Jesus to be a deceiver.

At issue was my demon-possessed son. Was he at fault? Why couldn't the disciples deliver him? The scribes blamed the disciples for their lack of power, and the crowd joined in the fray. Jesus' little flock was in total confusion, and I was caught in the middle.

The crowd, however, was more interested in seeing Jesus. In fact, "they were overwhelmed with wonder and ran to greet Him."

At the same time, Jesus appeared, with shining face, and asked, "What are you arguing with them about?" From the outset, Jesus questioned our discussion and noticed my dilemma. The dying embers of my hope were rekindled. So, I stepped forward and explained that my only son was afflicted by a spirit. In fact, the demon's control over my son rendered him unable to speak. I said, "Teacher, I brought you my son, who is possessed by a spirit that has robbed him of speech."

Since I was expecting deliverance for my son, I continued, "Whenever it seizes him, it throws him to the ground. He foams at the mouth, gnashes his teeth and becomes rigid. I asked your disciples to drive out the spirit, but they could not." I thought this could be the right opportunity to demean them and their Master.

Herbert Lockyer describes my son's condition as "lunatic" or "moonstruck," *luna* being the Latin word for *moon*. Epilepsy was believed to have been inflicted on persons who had sinned against the moon, and that changes in the moon governed their seizures.

This demon displayed itself in a major form of epilepsy, not simply a chronic nervous disorder. It was an attempt to destroy God's image in my son.

For whatever reason, the disciples failed to use the power Jesus had given them (Mark 3:15; 6:13). Would this failure disqualify them as Jesus' representatives? After all, as His followers, they were supposed to adhere to a basic principle of discipleship, "the messenger of a man is as the man himself."

Jesus was not disappointed with my unbelief and the disciples' failure, but with the critical scribes and unbelieving Israel.

Jesus said that unbelief and limited power are the results of an "unbelieving and perverse generation" (Luke 9:41). That is, He was ashamed of them. He wanted them to be different from men of the world who demand signs which do not respect God. The fact is, "If the disciples succeed, He succeeds; but if the disciples fail, Jesus fails."

At this point, Jesus commanded, "O unbelieving generation, how long shall I stay with you? How long shall I put up with you? Bring the boy to me." So, they brought my son to Jesus, and when the demon saw Jesus, "it immediately threw the boy into a convulsion. He fell to the ground and rolled around, foaming at the mouth."

Immediately, the demon recognized Jesus and became enraged. In its contempt for Jesus, the demon was extremely upset and angry. He was bent on destroying my son. James Hastings contended: "The cowardly fiend of hell assails the weak, because he would put an end to them before they get strong enough to do mischief to his kingdom."

When Jesus asked me, "How long has he been like this?" I replied, "From childhood."

This was an opportunity for me to express my feelings and unburden my heart. I was not trying to generate more faith, because no amount of faith can control God. After all, faith must never go beyond His promises. But, it must believe to receive what God has for them. In fact, if men have faith, there is no limit to what God will do for them.

In my distraught condition, I continued my plaintive plea, "It has often thrown him into fire or water to kill him. But if you can do anything, take pity on us and help us."

Interestingly, and probably providentially, others had already discovered that Jesus does *all* things well. That was the encouragement I needed.

At this point, my hope was hard to kill. As William Barclay explains, "To approach anything in the spirit of hopelessness is to make it hopeless; to approach anything in the spirit of faith is to make it a possibility."

By this time, my heart was breaking with grief, my mind was wrestling with doubt, and my son was on the ground, writhing in the grip of an evil spirit. I had said to Jesus, "if you can." Now, there is an *if* in Jesus' reply. His *if* is followed by a question, "If you can?" I had placed the *if* in the wrong place. But, Jesus explained, in the words of Charles H. Spurgeon, "There should be no 'if' about my power, nor concerning my willingness; the 'if' lies elsewhere. If you can believe, all things are possible to him who believes."

Spurgeon elaborates, "Faith stands in God's power and is robed in God's majesty; it wears the royal apparel and rides on the king's horse, for it is the grace which the king delights to honor. Girding itself with the glorious might of the all-working Spirit, faith becomes, in the omnipotence of God, power to do, to dare, and to suffer. All things, without limit, are possible to the one who believes."

Jesus knew He had power to heal my son, but did I have faith to believe it? After all, if I truly believe, I will not limit God's ability. Actually, when Jesus asked, "If you can?" He was placing my son's healing into my lap. Jesus had power to heal, but would I believe? All things are possible, but would I express my faith? Would I unite my faith with Jesus' power? Jesus was saying, "My action depends on your faith. That is, the degree to which I bless you depends on the degree of your faith."

Hardly able to contain my emotion and tears, I immediately shouted, "I do believe; help me overcome my unbelief!"

Os Guinness says, "to believe is to be 'in one mind' about accepting something as true; to disbelieve is to be 'in one mind' about rejecting it. To doubt is to waver between the two, to believe and doubt at once, and so to be 'in two minds.'" In effect, I was saying, "Lord, one part of me believes, another part doesn't. Help the part that doesn't."

I was keenly aware of my weakness, and saw my faith as lacking something. I believed but, being human, I needed stability where my faith wavered. After all, faith cannot be partial, but totally focussed and committed. So, I hoped Jesus would assist me to overcome my unbelief. I felt my unbelief as much as I felt my belief. But it was my belief which cried out for Jesus' help. I knew what I wanted and I knew it is better to confess wavering faith than to conceal it. So, I would tell my doubts to Jesus, and show my faith to others. This is faith which rests firmly in Jesus Christ.

By this time, the crowd had increased substantially. So, to avoid unnecessary publicity, Jesus rebuked the evil spirit and expelled it from my son. Besides, Jesus did not heal people simply to thrill the crowds. His purpose was to get me to know my need, feel my helpless misery and cling to Him for refuge.

When Jesus commanded the deaf and mute spirit to leave my son, "The spirit shrieked, convulsed him violently and came out. The boy looked so much like a corpse that many said, 'He's dead.'"

Jesus instructed the evil spirit to come out and warned it not to enter my boy again. Indeed, His power is universal – over people, nature, demons. With the Lord of Life present, the demon had met its match. With the Healer of Diseases present, the demon could not prevail. He had bruised the heel, but the demon would soon lose its head!

"But Jesus took him by the hand and lifted him to his feet, and he stood up." With the demon's last attack spoiled, in an act of triumph, Jesus took my son's hand and lifted him to his feet. I could not doubt Jesus' compassion and power. My faith had grasped His omnipotence!

It was obvious Jesus had demonstrated absolute power over the minds of the scribes and the rage of demons. And, since He has not changed, He provides rest to the heavy laden, in the words of James Hastings, "from perturbing thoughts, rest from tormenting uncertainties, rest from harassing doubts, as well as rest from weariness, and weakness, and wickedness." It was this majestic power of Christ which drew me to lay hold of His omnipotence.

When Jesus and the disciples went indoors, they were quick to ask Him privately, "Why couldn't we drive it out?" He replied, "This kind can come out only by prayer."

Jesus explained that because there are different kinds of demons, prayer is always required to expel them. That is, the power of Jesus is a must, and should not be taken for granted. Besides, difficult situations call for specific preparation like fasting and self-denial. Sometimes our bodies may need particular foods, or we may have to refrain from a certain food. While nothing is impossible with God, our faith must equal the need.

When it comes to our prayers, God does not require a specific quantity, a precise eloquence, a maximum length, or even scientific logic. But, He always expects faith. In fact, it is our faith that prays! A. B. Simpson expressed it like this:

Oh, how sweet the glorious message simple faith may claim:
Yesterday, today, forever, Jesus is the same;
Still He loves to save the sinful, heal the sick and lame,
Cheer the mourner, still the tempest – glory to His name!

19

Deliverance from Disbelief

The Man Born Blind
Mark 10:46-52

My story begins with a parade passing through Jericho, fifteen miles from Jerusalem and five miles west of the Jordan River. The parade is really a procession of pilgrims following Jesus on His way to the annual Passover Feast. The Law said that all males over twelve must attend.

As the crowd left the city, they encountered a blind man, begging by the side of the road, near the northern gate. I am a blind man, Bartimaeus, son of Timaeus. Both of us were well known in Jericho.

When the Israelites entered Canaan, God told them to destroy the city of Jericho. So, they walked around it once a day for a week. On the seventh day, they marched around the walls seven times. At the seventh time, the priests blew their horns and the walls collapsed. Then God warned them never to rebuild the city.

Years later, however, contrary to God's warning and curse, King Herod the Great built a summer palace near old Jericho. This became the new Jericho, where beggars of all kinds lined the road begging for handouts.

While Jericho's population was about 100,000, it had one unique feature – over 20,000 priests were involved in the Temple. They were divided into twenty-six groups to serve in rotation.

Hearing the crowd's unusual commotion, I was told Jesus of Nazareth was passing by. I lost no time in shouting, "Jesus. Son of David, have mercy on me!" From most reports, I heard He was the promised Messiah, who had power to heal all kinds of diseases. So, I began a relentless cry because I was convinced that if He could bring blessing to Israel, He could restore my sight.

The title, *Son of David*, was not new because many in Israel acknowledged Jesus' Messiahship as the future king of Israel, the descendent of David and the great expected Prophet (Ezek. 34:23-24). In fact, some, including me, believed that at His coming He would open the eyes of the blind (Isa. 29:18; 35:5). So, being an Israelite, I was justified in asking the king in David's line to give me sight.

Just as quickly, some in the crowd rebuked me and scolded me to shut up. But, I was desperate and roared all the more, "Son of David, have mercy on me!" I knew myself and I knew I needed mercy, God's kind!

My cries were so loud and annoying that they caught Jesus' attention. In fact, my words had an Old Testament ring to them, "Son of David, have mercy on me!" I did not know about Jesus, but I believed I could receive God's wonderful mercy from Him.

I was well known in Jericho because I usually sat in my regular spot by the roadside. Besides, people were familiar with my pleas for coins. Begging was my trade. I had asked for alms for years. It was my way of living.

Surprise! Surprise! Jesus stopped and commanded, "Call him." David J. Logan comments: "What wonderful words! 'Jesus stood still.' The pleading cries of the desperate blind man were ignored by most of the passing throng; others ordered him to be quiet. But 'Jesus stood still, and commanded him to be called.' In an impersonal world of electronic answering devices (leave your name, number and message); in a world of people who are too busy or consider themselves too important to take time for others, it is heartening to know that today as always, Jesus stands still for us. 'The Lord is nigh unto all them that call upon Him' (Ps. 145:18)."

When Jesus heard my call for help, He knew I was not asking for His money, but for His mercy to cure my blindness. Remember, Jesus was on His way to the cross, yet He stopped to help me in my distress. As R. Kent Hughes writes, "The heart's cry of one in need is far sweeter to Christ than the shallow hallelujahs of the crowd."

At first, when I called Jesus for help, the crowd tried to silence me. But, when Jesus said, "Call him," the crowd encouraged me to respond, "Cheer up! On your feet! He's calling you."

My personal appeal paid off. I could hardly believe it. Jesus called me and the crowd encouraged me. So, I flung my cloak aside, jumped to my feet and headed toward Jesus' voice, as the crowd cleared a path for my pursuit. Isn't it interesting how, in the words of David L. McKenna, "Posture always gives clues to self-esteem"?

My cloak served two purposes: for warmth and to spread in front of me to catch the coins of the travelling public. But, I discarded it in anticipation of not needing it anymore. Besides, I did not want anything to hinder me from getting to Jesus. Who knows? Jesus may never pass this way again.

Faith in Christ had made this blind sinner whole, and we read, "Immediately he received his sight and followed Jesus along the road." Obviously I came to Jesus at the right time, because we do not know if Jesus ever walked that way again.

It seems Jesus was as anxious to heal me as I was to receive my healing. When He asked, "What do you want me to do for you?" I replied, "Rabbi, I want to see."

My request was simple, but desperate. It was a call ready to receive an answer. I felt I was expressing the soul of humanity struggling for light from the One who would "open eyes that are blind ... and to release from the dungeon those who sit in darkness" (Isa. 42:7).

The fact is, I knew I wanted healing and I knew who would heal me. And, I knew my Greek name, Timao, means *honor*. So, in the future, instead of a "son of honor" begging beside the road, I would let Jesus restore my sight forever!

Then Jesus commanded, "Go, your faith has healed you." Yes, it was immediate. My eyes were opened. I would now follow Jesus to the Temple and offer a sacrifice of thanksgiving for my sight.

I know my cries annoyed the crowd, but I caught Jesus' attention. Let the crowd refuse to call, if they want. Let them say "God is dead," if they want. All I know is, once I was blind, now I see. To me, Jesus is not a dead Christ we should casually remember. Rather, He is the living Christ, moving among us, building His Church and administering the affairs of the universe. In fact, "Christ is the healing power of the world. And just as he heals our bodies, he can miraculously heal our broken hearts. When we surrender our hurts to him, he mysteriously works within our thoughts and feelings to set us free."

Longfellow describes Bartimaeus' miracle like this:

Blind Bartimaeus at the gates
Of Jericho in darkness waits:
He hears the crowd; he hears a breath
Say, "It is Christ of Nazareth!"
And calls in tones of agony,
"O Jesus, Jesus, pity me!"

The thronging multitudes increase –
"Blind Bartimaeus, hold thy peace!"
But still, above the noisy crowd,
The blind man's cry is shrill and loud:
Until they say, "He calleth thee;
Courage! Arise! He calleth thee!"

Then saith the Christ, as silent stands
The crowd, "What wilt thou at My hands?"
And he replies, "O give me light! Rabbi,
Restore the blind man's sight."
And Jesus answers, "Go thy way,
Thy faith, thy faith hath saved thee."

Ye that have eyes and cannot see,
In darkness and in misery,
Recall those mighty voices three –
"O Jesus, Jesus, pity me!"
"Courage! Arise! He calleth thee!"
"Thy faith, thy faith hath saved thee."

20

Deliverance for the Distraught

The Crippled Woman
Luke 13:10-17

My story of deliverance took place in a Jewish synagogue on the Sabbath – an ideal day and place for a miracle. It represents Israel's freedom from merciless bondage to legalism.

On this Sabbath, Jesus was teaching in one of Jerusalem's 400 synagogues.

I am well known, especially in our local synagogue. I have been a cripple for eighteen years. That is, I am bent over, and because my spine is so fused, I am unable to stand erect. To do so is considered man's honour above beasts. But, my physical ailment was caused by an evil spirit. Some believe my infirmity was my punishment from God. But, no, it was not my choice. While the evil spirit did not *possess* me, it certainly *oppressed* me – in my body, but not in my mind. Today, my physical condition is known as a curvature or a dislocation of the vertebrae of the spine. Simply put, I was deformed. Disabled.

While I did not make an appeal for my deliverance, my healing was instantaneous. It happened while Jesus taught. He took the first step and called me to come to Him, saying, "Woman, you are set free from your infirmity." This was my miracle of mercy. Jesus simply flung off my oppression and replaced it with the glory of God.

I was pleasantly surprised because He did not have to expel a demon. He simply delivered me from my spinal condition.

When Jesus laid His hands on me, I received His strength and felt my back unfolding. I immediately stood straight and began to praise God. Obviously, Jesus' hand terrifies and expels oppressing spirits.

However, not everyone was happy with my healing, at least not on the Sabbath. The synagogue official, a narrow-minded Pharisee, was very indignant that Jesus healed me on this sacred day. This Pharisee was responsible for supervising all teaching in the synagogue. So, according to him, Jesus was out of order. Apparently, the spirit afflicting me was now controlling him.

This official was critical of me for coming to the synagogue to be healed on the Sabbath, and critical of Jesus for healing or working on the Sabbath. He claimed that six work days were long enough for someone to be healed.

According to Jewish traditional laws, medicine and healing were illegal on the Sabbath. Herbert Lockyer states, "When God prescribed the Sabbath for man, forbidding him to work therein, He did not thereby bind His own hands and make it improper for Himself to work, mercifully, on that day. As the Lord of the Sabbath, nothing, not even such a day, can stay Him in His ministry of grace and power."

To paraphrase Jesus' logical rebuke, J. Willcock writes: "You reproach the people, but your quarrel is really with Me. You pretend to be zealous for the law, but you are only jealous of My work. You Pharisees deserve no credit for even conscientiously mistaken views about the sanctity of the seventh day. Your ideas of its observance are quite sane and sensible so soon as a question arises affecting your own material interests. You would have no scruples in relieving the wants of a suffering animal on that day by a certain amount of Sabbath labour. But when I loose from long years of Satanic bondage one of your human sisters, a daughter of the chosen family, and do it with no labour at all, you are filled with horror at the breach of the Sabbath law."

Jesus concluded His rebuke with this Scripture, "You hypocrites! Doesn't each of you on the Sabbath untie his ox or donkey from the stall and lead it out to give it water?"

With His superior logic, Jesus explained to the congregation that Scripture does not forbid watering animals or healing the sick on the Sabbath. In fact, He said that only hypocrites place a higher value on animals than on people. Like the formal Pharisees, they had zeal for the Law, but no concern for a person's healing. Jesus, however, put people first and laws second. In my case, my healing was an obligation.

According to A. B. Bruce, "The Sabbath is meant to be a blessing to mankind, not a burden. It is not a day taken from us by God in an exacting spirit, but a day given by God in mercy to man – God's holiday for His subjects. Take Christ's view, and your principle becomes: The best way of observing the Sabbath is that which is most conducive to my spiritual and physical well being – in other words, what is best for my body and soul. In the light of this principle, you will keep the holy day in the spirit of intelligent joy and thankfulness to the Creator."

I was a kindred spirit with Abraham. In coming to my defence, Jesus called me a Jewish daughter of Abraham, a friend of God, just as much as Zaccheus was the son of Abraham (Luke 19:9). He said Satan had bound me for eighteen years, and that I should be delivered as soon as possible, regardless of the day. As a daughter of Abraham, I was one of the inner circle of pious Jews "waiting for the consolation of Israel" (Luke 2:25). I was, therefore, entitled to Messiah's blessings.

The fact is, as Satan was permitted to attack Job, so God allowed Satan to attack me. It was not because of any personal sin, but all for God's glory. Besides, why should I continue for another day to be bound by Satan's power when God's power was available and working? Why not deliver me by God's power, on His day and in His house? After all, relieving human sorrow is always current.

As Jesus spoke, His critics became humiliated. The congregation, however, liked what they heard and began to rejoice because of how Jesus delivered me.

I was convinced, in the words of S. Gillies, that God's kingdom "is a powerful agency for deliverance, and will overcome the kingdom of Satan and its power, as Jesus demonstrated."

Jessie B. Pounds could relate to my experience in her poem, *The Touch of His Hand on Mine.*

There are days so dark that I seek in vain
For the face of my friend divine;
But though darkness hide, He is there to guide
By the touch of His hand on mine.

CHORUS:
Oh, the touch of His hand on mine,
Oh, the touch of His hand on mine,
There is grace and power, in the trying hour,
In the touch of His hand on mine.

There are times, when tired of the toilsome road,
That for ways of the world I pine;
But He draws me back to the upward track
By the touch of His hand on mine.

When the way is dim, and I cannot see
Through the mist of His wise design,
How my glad heart yearns and my faith returns
By the touch of His hand on mine.

In the last sad hour, as I stand alone,
Where the powers of death combine,
While the dark waves roll He will guide my soul
By the touch of His hand on mine.

21

Deliverance from Dropsy

The Unknown Man
Luke 14:1-4

Dropsy, or edema, is the result of a build up of fluid, mainly water. It accumulates in the tissues, affecting the kidneys and liver, causing the neck, arms and legs to swell like balloons.

That's what I had. Rather, that's what had me. I was afflicted with dropsy.

I was a real character with a real story. It happened in a prominent Pharisee's house where Jesus and I were invited for a festive meal, and it was on the Sabbath.

Luke records five of Jesus' *Sabbath* miracles, while John records the other two.

I said Jesus and I were invited. That may be so for Jesus, but I was likely the *guinea pig* used to trap Jesus. As Luke indicates, Jesus "was being carefully watched." There I was, an unnamed visitor, like bait in a trap, deliberately placed in front of Jesus. No doubt, members of the Sanhedrin could not wait to get a report from their *watchdog* at the table.

Jesus saw me and knew the intent of the setup. His direct question was, "Is it lawful to heal on the Sabbath or not?" This question was quite legitimate. After all, Jesus liked doing good on the Sabbath. Besides, when it comes to helping and healing, "no Sabbath law, no so-called religious restriction, can ever forbid helping the miserable."

However, Jesus had those Pharisees and experts of the Law cornered. In fact, they were powerless. They could not object or protest afterward. They had no grounds against healing on the Sabbath. So, they sat in stony, sulky silence.

Instead of trapping Jesus, they trapped themselves. "If they had said that healing on the Sabbath was not permissible, they would have condemned themselves; if they had said that it was, they could not have criticised him."

Strange, isn't it? The Pharisees had no hesitation about feasting on the Sabbath, but healing the sick on the Sabbath was unthinkable and unforgiveable (Mark 3:1-6).

There are two versions of the Ten Commandments, one in Exodus 20 and the other in Deuteronomy 5. The only Commandment that changes significantly concerns the Sabbath. According to the Exodus version, failing to keep the Sabbath threatens God's creation intentions. In Deuteronomy 5, however, the Sabbath marks Israel's redemptive release from Pharaoh's bondage. So, all redemptive action on the Sabbath, like healing, would be acceptable.

When Jesus had seen and heard enough, He healed me. "So taking hold of the man, he healed him and sent him away."

Alexander Maclaren comments: "Silently he comes on stage, silently he gets his blessing, silently he disappears. A strange, sad instance of how possible it is to have a momentary connection with Jesus, and even to receive gifts from His hand, and yet to have no real, permanent relation to Him!"

My healing caused me to adopt this conclusion: "In the kingdom of God, under the royal law, works of necessity and of mercy are always right – the former because the day of rest was ordained for the benefit of man, not for his hurt, and the second because the Divine love never ceases its activities."

As for the dropsy, it is considered to be somehow connected to an organic disease. However, Jesus displayed His compassion by touching me and healing me. This shows the love of His heart toward human hurt. As He lived to relieve the afflicted, so he died to deliver everybody from sin. He gave His life to pay for our sin and rose again to give us new life, eternal life. May you acknowledge Him as your Deliverer!

Afterword

After Jesus' ascension, various healings and other miracles became normal in the first church. On the Day of Pentecost, the miracle of other languages spread throughout Jerusalem. Then, through Peter and John, a crippled man received healing and he joined others to worship God in the Temple.

In his book, *Simply Jesus*, N. T. Wright comments, "Stories abound of changed lives, of physical and emotional healing. New churches have sprung up, full of eager and excited people, often young people. Addicts are cured. Dysfunctional families are reunited. Real help is given to the sick, the poor, the prisoners. Failing schools are turned around. New energy is found for creative social and cultural projects. For such people, the whole thing is real enough. It's hard to argue with a radically changed life or, indeed, with still being alive when the doctors had given you up for dead."

Ronald A. N. Kydd testifies, "First, it is clear to me that the restoration of health through the direct intervention of God has continued throughout the history of the church, and at no point has it been any more widely seen than it is now."

The Apostle Paul highlights the Holy Spirit's ministry by providing believers with a) establishment gifts (Eph. 4:11-13), b) edification gifts (1 Cor. 12-14), and c) extension gifts (Rom. 12:1-8). While Jesus' miracles were not done in isolation, neither is His ongoing ministry in believers through the Church. Consequently, the work of the Apostles "was not done in a corner" (Acts 26:26).

As for our sickness and suffering, much of it is the result of our own wrongdoing. When Jesus healed the man by the pool of Bethesda, He warned him, "See, you are well again. Stop sinning or something worse may happen to you" (John 5:14). Again, because Miriam and Aaron refused to submit to Moses' leadership, God afflicted Miriam with leprosy (Num. 12:10). However, sickness because of sin can be remedied by confession, and one can be healed by the prayer of faith. Then, the anointing with oil declares him fit to be part of a local body of believers (James 5:13-16). On the other hand, as in the case of the man born blind, sin does not have anything to do with sickness. Jesus explained to His disciples, "Neither this man nor his parents sinned, but this happened so that the work of God might be displayed in his life" (John 9:3).

Brother Lawrence wrote: "God is often (in some sense) nearer to us and more effectually present with us, in sickness than in health …. He often sends diseases of the body to cure those of the soul. Comfort yourself with the sovereign Physician of both the soul and body."

Although Jesus healed scores of people, He said very little about the sickness or the healing. A history of the sickness did not add anything to the cure. His miracle was more important than the diagnosis. Whether the cause was bodily neglect, personal sin or an evil force in the world, Jesus came "that they may have life, and have it to the full" (John 10:10). Kydd quotes Morton Kelsey, "If Jesus had any one mission, it was to bring the power and healing of God's creative, loving spirit to bear upon the moral, mental and physical illnesses of the people around him."

The question often arises, "What is the basis for divine healing?" Speaking prophetically, Isaiah declared, "by his wounds we are healed" (53:5). In other words, divine healing is directly related to Christ's suffering and death, that is, His atonement. However, J. Sidlow Baxter contends "that one should talk about healing as occurring *through* the atonement rather than being *in* the atonement." The fact is, Jesus *took up* our infirmities, that is, He bore our sin and sickness, similar to the priests who carried "the vessels of the Lord" (Isa. 52:11). God is well able to provide direct healing in answer to prayer or sufficient grace to meet whatever physical need we have in a way that honours Him (2 Cor. 12:7-9).

It follows, then, that Jesus is superior to disease and death. His very presence lends hope to the worst situation. And, according to J. Wilkinson, "faith was never asked for as a condition for healing." Jesus did not ask for faith when He healed Peter's mother-in-law of a fever (Matt. 8:14). He knew she trusted Him totally. Apparently, her healing did not depend on her, but on Him.

While Jesus is at the centre of all healings, what role does the Holy Spirit play? Being the agent of our salvation (John 3:5-8; 1 Cor. 12:13), He is also the agent of our healing, usually through the gift of faith, gifts of healing and working of miracles (1 Cor. 12; 14).

The New Testament shows Jesus' healing ministry as an integral part of His total work. His healings and miracles were not side issues, but vital physical and spiritual aspects to redeem man's full personality. In fact, when He commissioned His disciples, He sent them to preach and heal (Mark 3:15; Luke 10:9).

Why did Jesus heal the sick? To prove His deity? No. He actually avoided fame and attention. He often said, "See that you don't tell anyone" (Matt. 8:4). The point is, Jesus did not want to use miracles to draw people to Him. He did not operate by emotion and dramatic works. His methods were holiness and love. Besides, miracles do not create belief for salvation (Luke 16:31).

Jesus healed the sick for three reasons. First, He had compassion for hurting people. He did not touch lepers and take children in His arms to amaze the spectators. In fact, when He saw the afflicted, He suffered with them (Isa. 53:4; Matt. 8:17). Second, Jesus healed the sick because, to Him, disease was an intruder in people's lives. It was alien and foreign to God's kingdom. So, Jesus came out of heaven because things were wrong with the world. Third, Jesus healed the sick to destroy the works of Satan.

You see, in Jesus' day, disease was considered to be the work of demons. So, every healing or miracle meant that good was victorious and Satan's kingdom was being shaken and falling apart.

Often, the question arises as to how Jesus performed healings and miracles. He healed through His sinlessness, not through any magic, but through His moral life. So, because of such pure character, His healings are not surprising. Indeed, the impact of His resurrection enhanced the fact that He was a conqueror before whom disease and death must submit (Acts 2:24). Also, Jesus healed through His faith in God. God the Father answered Jesus' prayers because of His faith. But, like the disciples, we are sometimes powerless because of our unbelief (Matt. 17:20). In addition, Jesus healed through man's faith in God. Miracles were scarce where faith was scarce (Matt. 13:58). Finally, Jesus healed because the power of God was present to heal (John 3:34).

When it comes to present-day dilemmas, cancer has to be our worst nightmare. We refer to it as *the plague*. My high school teacher in the late 1950's, and respected friend, Ronald Clarke, comments: "In any case, if I have to face real cancer I certainly do NOT have to face it alone! I believe in Jesus Christ, my Saviour, my brother. Jesus is stronger than cancer, or any other 'fatal' disease ... So, why should I be afraid? All of us must truly believe in Jesus, and claim Him as our Saviour. If we truly TRUST him, nothing really bad can happen to us. ALLELUIA!"

Works Cited

Augsburger, Myron S. *Matthew*. The Communicator's Commentary, gen. ed., Lloyd J. Ogilvie. Waco, TX: Word, 1982.

Barclay, William. *The Gospel of Mark*. The Daily Study Bible. Burlington, ON: G. R. Welch, revised 1975.

Barker, Kenneth (gen. ed.). *The NIV Study Bible: New International Version*. Grand Rapids, MI: Zondervan, 1985.

Barnes, Albert. "Commentary." 2015. Online posting. 2014 <http://www.e-sword.net/>

Baxter, J. Sidlow. *Divine Healing of the Body*. Grand Rapids, MI: Zondervan, 1979.

Bosch, Henry G. "The Power of the Gospel." *Our Daily Bread*. 23 May 1992.

Brother Lawrence. *The Practice of the Presence of God*. Radford, VA: Wilder, 2008.

Bruce, A. B. *Loaves and Fishes*.

Bruce, F. F. *The Gospel of John: Introduction, Exposition and Notes*. Grand Rapids, MI: Eerdmans, 1983.

Bruner, Frederick Dale. *The Christbook: A Historical/Theological Commentary. Matthew 1-12*. Waco, TX: Word, 1987.

Burdick, Donald W. "Mark," in *The Wycliffe Bible Commentary*, eds., Charles F. Pfeiffer and Everett F. Harrison. Chicago, IL: Moody, 1962.

Clarke, Ron. "The BIG 'C.'" *Anglican Life*. June 2014.

Collins, Velma D. "The Second Touch." *Pentecostal Evangel*.

Craddock, Fred B. *Luke*. Interpretation: A Bible Commentary for Teaching and Preaching, eds., James Luther Mays and Paul J. Achtemeier. Louisville, KY: Westminster John Knox, 2009.

Exley, Richard. *Encounters With Christ: Experience the Miracles and Transforming Power of an Unexpected Savior*. Lakeland, FL: White Stone Books, 2005.

Gariepy, Henry. *Christianity in Action: The International History of The Salvation Army*. Grand Rapids, MI: Eerdmans, 2009.

Gill, John. "Exposition on the Whole Bible." 2015. Online posting. 2014 <http://www.e-sword.net/>

Gillies, S. *Daily Notes*. 1993.

Gooding, David. *According to Luke: A New Exposition of the Third Gospel*. Leicester, England: Inter-Varsity; Grand Rapids, MI: Eerdmans, 1987.

Guinness, Os. In *Our Daily Bread*.

Harrison, Everett F. "John," in *The Wycliffe Bible Commentary*, eds., Charles F. Pfeiffer and Everett F. Harrison. Chicago, IL: Moody, 1982.

Hastings, James (ed.). *The Great Texts of the Bible: St. Mark*. New York: Charles Scribner's Sons; Edinburgh: T. & T. Clark, 1910.

Hughes, R. Kent. *Mark: Jesus, Servant and Savior*, vol. 1. Preaching the Word. Westchester, IL: Crossway, 1989.

---------------. *Mark: Jesus, Servant and Savior*, vol. 2. Preaching the Word. Westchester, IL: Crossway, 1989.

Kent, Homer A., Jr. *Light in the Darkness: Studies in the Gospel of John*. Winona Lake, IN: BMH Books, second ed., 2005.

---------------. "Matthew," in *The Wycliffe Bible Commentary*, eds., Charles F. Pfeiffer and Everett F. Harrison. Chicago, IL: Moody, 1962.

Kistemaker, Simon J. *The Miracles: Exploring the Mystery of Jesus's Divine Works*. Grand Rapids, MI: Baker Books, 2006.

Kydd, Ronald A. N. *Healing Through the Centuries: Models for Understanding*. Peabody, MA: Hendrickson, 1998.

Lane, William L. *The Gospel of Mark*. The New International Commentary on the New Testament, gen. ed., F. F. Bruce. Grand Rapids, MI: Eerdmans, 1974.

Lang, G. H. *Pictures and Parables: Studies in the Parabolic Teaching of Holy Scripture*. London: Paternoster, 1955.

Liefeld, Walter L. "Luke," in *The Expositor's Bible Commentary*. Eds., Frank E. Gaebelein and J. D. Douglas. Grand Rapids, MI: Zondervan, 1984.

Littleton, Mark R. *Herald of Holiness*.

Lloyd, Michael. *Café Theology: Exploring Love, the Universe and Everything*. London: Alpha, 2005.

Lockyer, Herbert. *All the Miracles of the Bible: The Supernatural in Scripture: Its Scope and Significance*. Grand Rapids, MI: Zondervan, 1961.

Logan, David J. *Gleanings calendar*.

Longfellow, Henry Wadsworth. "Blind Bartimaeus." (Public Domain)

Maclaren, Alexander. *The Gospel According to St. Matthew Chapters IX to XVII*. Expositions of Holy Scripture. New York: A. C. Armstrong & Son; London: Hodder and Stoughton, 1905.

--------------. *The Gospel According to St. Mark Chapters I to VIII*. Expositions of Holy Scripture. London: Hodder and Stoughton, 1906.

--------------. *The Gospel According to St. Luke Chapters I to XII*. Expositions of Holy Scripture. London: Hodder and Stoughton, 1908.

--------------. *The Gospel According to St. John Chapters I to VIII*. Expositions of Holy Scripture. London: Hodder and Stoughton, 1907.

--------------, cited in *Loaves and Fishes*, 1993.

Martin, Allan. *Daily Notes*. 1993.

McKenna, David L. *Mastering the New Testament: Mark*. The Communicator's Commentary, gen. ed., Lloyd J. Ogilvie. Dallas, TX: Word, 1982.

McKenzie, Alyce M. *Matthew*. Interpretation Bible Studies. Louisville, KY: Westminster John Knox, 2002.

Meyer, F. B. in *Loaves and Fishes*.

Morgan, G. Campbell. *The Great Physician: The Method of Jesus With Individuals*. Old Tappan, NJ: Fleming H. Revell, 1937.

Morris, Leon. *Reflections on the Gospel of John: The Word Was Made Flesh John 1-5*, vol. 1. Grand Rapids, MI: Baker, 1986.

Nickle, Keith F. *Preaching the Gospel of Luke: Proclaiming God's Royal Rule*. Louisville, KY: Westminster John Knox, 2000.

Parker, Joseph. *The People's Bible: Discourses Upon Holy Scripture*, vol. XXI (Mark-Luke). New York: Funk & Wagnalls, n. d.

---------------. *The People's Bible: Discourses Upon Holy Scripture,* vol. XXII (John). New York: Funk & Wagnalls, n. d.

Phillips, John. *Exploring the Gospels: John*. Neptune, NJ: Loizeaux, 1988.

Pounds, Jessie B. "The Touch of His Hand on Mine."

Redding, David A. *The Miracles of Christ*. Westwood, NJ: Fleming H. Revell, 1964.

Renner, Rick. *Sparkling Gems from the Greek: 365 Greek Word Studies for Every Day of the Year To Sharpen Your Understanding of God's Word*. Tulsa, OK: Teach All Nations, 2003.

Scroggie, W. Graham. Source unknown.

Simpson, A. B. "Yesterday, Today, Forever."

Spurgeon, C. H. *Loaves and Fishes*. 16-17 November 1991.

Stafford, Tim. *Miracles: A Journalist Looks at Modern-Day Experiences of God's Power*. Minneapolis, MN: Bethany House, 2012.

Summers, Ray. *Commentary on Luke: Jesus, the Universal Savior*. Waco, TX: Word, 1972.

Telford, George B., Jr. Source unknown.

Tenney, Merrill C. "Luke," in *The Wycliffe Bible Commentary*, eds., Charles F. Pfeiffer and Everett F. Harrison. Chicago, IL: Moody, 1962.

Trench, Richard Chenevix. *Notes on the Miracles of our Lord*. Twin Brooks Series. Grand Rapids, MI: Baker, 1949.

Walker, Thomas W. *Luke*. Interpretation Bible Studies. Louisville, KY: Westminster John Knox, 2001.

Wilkinson, J. "Study of Healing in the Gospel According to John," *Scottish Journal of Theology* 20 (1967).

Willcock, J. *A Homiletical Commentary on the Gospel According to St. Luke*. The Preacher's Complete Homiletical Commentary on the New Testament. New York: Funk & Wagnalls, 1896.

Wright, N. T. *Simply Jesus: A New Vision of Who He Was, What He Did, and Why He Matters*. New York: HarperCollins, 2011.

Acknowledgments

Most writing projects require a certain amount of research. In my Works Cited, I recognize and appreciate many authors. Others are unknown, but their material is relevant. If I have missed any, I will give proper credit in any future edition.

For this venture, I am grateful for freelance editor, Burton K. Janes. As an accomplished author, his editing and formatting abilities were extremely helpful. When it comes to writing, Burton knows his lines.

For the final touches to the manuscript, I solicited the assistance of Karen Janes Winsor. Being meticulous for details, she checked references, corrected punctuation and revised sentence structure, to my delight.

Fortunately, I have three positive siblings, Judy, Roy and Ron, who always appreciate my writing endeavours, as well as find tangible ways to help.

Elliott Baker has been my close colleague since 1960. We have studied together, shared pulpits, picked pears, packed groceries, sorted mail and quelled student rivalry; and through it all, laughed our way to survival, without any rehearsal.

Ronald Clarke, my favourite high school teacher, taught by attitude and example. I enjoyed his Art, English and Religion classes. More than that, I appreciate him as a dependable friend.

I am very pleased for the moral and prayerful support of my wife, Laura, who obviously believed in this project. Our four children, Barbara Freake, Michael, Tina Strutt and Richard, offered their smiles of approval and words of encouragement. Such family favour makes a writing father extremely happy.